Sally Welch is Associate Vicar of St Margaret's Church, North Oxford, working clc
She leads an enthusiastic toddler group, a thriving Sunday school, a music sch
monthly activity morning on a Saturday, where her craft activities are trialled.

Sally is also Spirituality Adviser for the Diocese of Oxford and a contributor to BRF's spirituality resource, *Quiet Spaces*. Her published works are *Making a Pilgrimage* (Lion Hudson, 2009), *Walking the Labyrinth* (Canterbury Press, 2010) and *Every Place is Holy Ground* (Canterbury Press, 2011).

Important Information

Photocopying permission

The Copyright Licensing Agency (CLA)

Barnabas
for
Children®

Barnabas for Children® is a registered word mark and the logo is a registered device mark of The Bible Reading Fellowship.

Text copyright © Sally Welch 2014
Photographs copyright © Sally Welch 2014
The author asserts the moral right
to be identified as the author of this work

Published by
The Bible Reading Fellowship
15 The Chambers, Vineyard
Abingdon OX14 3FE
United Kingdom
Tel: +44 (0)1865 319700
Email: enquiries@brf.org.uk
Website: www.brf.org.uk
BRF is a Registered Charity

ISBN 978 0 85746 243 5

First published 2014
10 9 8 7 6 5 4 3 2 1 0
All rights reserved

Acknowledgments
Unless otherwise stated, scripture quotations are taken from the New Revised Standard Version of the Bible, Anglicised edition, copyright © 1989, 1995 by the Division of Christian Education of the National Council of the Churches of Christ in the United States of America, and are used by permission. All rights reserved.

Scripture quotations taken from The Holy Bible, New International Version (Anglicised edition). Copyright © 1979, 1984, 2011 by Biblica (formerly International Bible Society). Used by permission of Hodder & Stoughton Publishers, an Hachette UK company. All rights reserved. 'NIV' is a registered trademark of Biblica (formerly International Bible Society). UK trademark number 1448790.

Bible story passages are taken from The Barnabas Children's Bible (Barnabas for Children, 2012) except where indicated. Used with permission.

A catalogue record for this book is available from the British Library.

Printed by Gutenberg Press, Tarxien, Malta.

Edible.
Bible Crafts

64 delicious story-based craft ideas for children

Sally Welch

To Jeremy, Jess, Si, Ellie and James, who had to guess the story, then eat the craft!

Acknowledgments

With grateful thanks to the families who attend SAMs, and the volunteers, especially Liz Holmes, who make it happen. Thanks also to Andrew Bunch, Vicar of St Margaret's, Oxford.

Contents

Foreword

I love Sally Welch's imagination. I had never thought of illustrating the great biblical stories through edible crafts and I'm not sure many others have, either. But Sally has proved just how effective this process is, combining learning, fun and fascinating food.

The Christian story no longer has the privileged place it used to have in our culture. Indeed, sometimes it seems to be slipping out of our cultural memory at an alarming rate. Yet people with Sally's powers of imagination are always finding new ways to tell the story. Art, music, film, drama, poetry, literature—all have been used for centuries and are forever developing new and exciting examples of their art-form. YouTube and video clips are newer expressions of the same creativity and are full of potential if we can release the energies of willing people with the necessary expertise.

But I'd never thought of cakes! Sally Welch was several steps ahead of me, of course, and the suggestions and examples in this book are the result of much fun-filled experimentation with her groups of children and families. To combine telling the story with making and eating it is a brilliant coup. Just to look at the examples here is to chuckle.

Judaism and Christianity are full of the significance of food and the act of eating together. From Adam and Eve's illicit picnic in Eden to the heavenly banquet in the teaching of Jesus, food is a constant theme. It's basic to every person's life and to every nation's flourishing. Sally couldn't have used a more fundamental medium through which to tell the story.

Have fun with the ideas in this book. Use and adapt them, as you would with all the best recipes. Don't tell my grandchildren, but they're about to help their grandfather in the kitchen. Do I hear 'About time!' from next door?

+John Pritchard, Bishop of Oxford

Introduction

● ●

And he said to me, 'Son of man, eat what is before you, eat this scroll; then go and speak to the people of Israel.' So I opened my mouth, and he gave me the scroll to eat. Then he said to me, 'Son of man, eat this scroll I am giving you and fill your stomach with it.' So I ate it, and it tasted as sweet as honey in my mouth. He then said to me: 'Son of man, go now to the people of Israel and speak my words to them.'

EZEKIEL 3:1–4 (NIV)

This book is intended for anyone who works with young children and is looking for an interesting way to share Bible stories with them. It developed out of my own work with a Saturday morning café in a city centre church. Tables and chairs were set up at the back of the church and families were invited in to enjoy a breakfast of croissants, pains au chocolat, fresh fruit, good coffee and orange juice. We provided a selection of the day's papers for the adults and seven or eight different craft activities for the children.

Very soon we realised that the parents enjoyed the craft activities as much as the children did, and that this was a precious opportunity for them to share an activity together. The church provided the activities, and volunteers did all the clearing up afterwards, so families could enjoy a number of crafts without having the burden of additional housework afterwards.

The most popular crafting activity was always the edible craft. Each month, a different Bible story was highlighted and the crafts developed around the theme. Telling the story as the craft was made became an important part of the morning, and the fact that the story could be 'eaten' afterwards made it all the better.

Sally Welch

The principles of edible Bible crafts

Bible-based

This book is designed for people working with families with young children, as a way of introducing them to some of the stories in the Bible. The sessions begin with a retelling of the Bible story, usually taken from *The Barnabas Children's Bible* (Barnabas for Children, 2012). Key verses from the story are shown underneath, in the New Revised Standard Version. The one exception is the Easter story (page 112), in which both the retelling and the key verses are taken from the New International Version. The sessions then encourage some reflection on an aspect of the story and, finally, enable families to enjoy working together to produce an edible illustration of the story.

Easy to construct

The crafts have all been tested in a church situation. They do not take very long to make and are simple enough for children aged eight or above to make by studying a finished example. Younger children will probably need some adult supervision, if only to ensure that they follow basic safety and hygiene rules, such as not putting knives into their mouths or licking the ends of writing icing tubes.

Very often, a valuable part of the edible craft activity is the enjoyment experienced by parents as they work with their children to craft something together, and many adults have reported that they themselves had never previously tried icing cakes or decorating biscuits and were delighted by the effects they produced.

No special equipment

None of the crafts uses elaborate equipment. The most sophisticated only require different shapes of cookie cutter, and, although an electric mixer is very useful if making lots of cakes or biscuits, it is not obligatory. A list of the basic equipment required can be found in the next chapter.

Limited preparation

There is some preparation required, but it does not take very long and is mostly limited to the mass production of plain fairy cakes and biscuits. If time is very limited, these basic components can be purchased at a supermarket, or alterative crafts can be chosen that use rice cakes or syrup pancakes as a base, rather than a home-made product. The crafts do not take very long to make, as the attention span of children can be limited.

No cooking during the craft session

Because most church craft activities take place in buildings with restricted facilities, there is no cooking involved during the craft session itself. For this reason, activities such as bread-making or biscuit-making are not included, as the logistics of baking are too great for smaller churches to accomplish easily. This also avoids many of the health and safety issues of cooking with young children, as well as the issue of how to fill the gap between the end of the craft and the time when it is ready to eat.

Organising edible craft activities for young children

● ●

Hygiene and food safety

When setting up edible craft sessions for children, hygiene and food safety are absolute priorities.

None of the recipes in this book contains nuts because these can produce the most violent allergic reactions (see 'Allergies and food intolerances'). They do not use raw egg or any food product that needs to be kept refrigerated at all times. If your craft sessions are taking place in a cold church building, the ambient room temperature will probably not be so high that special precautions are necessary to keep food cool. However, if your room is warm, take care not to bring out ingredients such as cheese or eggs until just before the start of the craft session.

None of the recipes uses food that has to be hot, so there should be no risk of burns or scalds.

Make sure that you have wiped every surface with antibacterial spray before setting up the craft. The best method is to cover your tables with banqueting paper, such as the sort used in industrial catering. This way, you can ensure that the surface is perfectly clean and also keep the clearing up to a minimum.

On every table, keep a supply of antibacterial wet wipes and encourage the children to use them frequently to wipe fingers and hands. Strongly discourage the licking of fingers, and even more strongly discourage the unconscious tendency for writing icing tubes, icing knives and other implements to find their way into toddlers' mouths.

There should also be a bottle of antibacterial hand cleanser on every table. Every child should use it at the beginning of the session and again every time they return to the edible craft table, having been away from it for however short a time. At the end of the session, children should be encouraged to clean their hands again with the hand cleanser.

Food crafting equipment should be kept separately from other craft supplies. Scissors and knives should be bought and used only for food and stored in airtight boxes. Other equipment should be safely stored in airtight containers.

Allergies and food intolerances

Many children suffer from one of a range of food allergies and intolerances, and one danger when working with very young children and food is that these allergies may not yet have manifested themselves. Nuts can provoke particularly severe reactions, so there are no nuts or nut products used in any of these recipes.

When baking, take care that the kitchen is entirely clear of nuts or nut products, as even using a chopping board that has been previously used for nuts can provoke a reaction.

Other allergens, such as wheat and egg, can be avoided either by using the gluten and egg-free recipes or by using an alternative such as rice cakes or biscuits instead of cakes.

When working with children who have a known food allergy, great care must be taken to avoid cross-contamination—for example, knives being used to cut cakes and then spread icing on biscuits. If a child has a particularly severe allergy, it might be best to ensure that the entire craft is free from the allergen, rather than restricting the child to a particular part of the craft or placing them on a separate table.

Equipment required

In the kitchen

- Cake racks for cooling cakes. Buy enough racks to cool a batch of cakes. If you are cooking 36 cakes at a time, you will need two or three racks.
- Cake tins for small and medium-sized fairy cakes. The tins do not need to be expensive: the cheapest ones your supermarket can provide are absolutely fine. Buy as many as you have shelves in your oven; that way, you can be economical with your electricity and cook 24 or 36 cakes at a time.
- Paper cake cases. I have found that the very cheap cases come away from the cake mixture during the cooking process and look rather untidy at the end. It is better to opt for a mid-range case, such as those made by Dr Oetker, which are widely available. Don't buy large or muffin cases: they either use too much batter or look half empty when they are cooked.
- A sharp knife.
- An electric mixer or food blender. While not absolutely necessary, either of these will save you a lot of hard work. Again, they do not have to be expensive. I use a supermarket 'value' electric mixer and it is fine.
- Baking parchment. This is a vital piece of kitchen equipment for rolling out biscuit dough, fondant icing and so on. Buy in large quantities, as you will need a lot.
- A rolling pin.

For crafting

- Blunt-ended knives.
- Flower- and star-shaped cookie cutters in at least two sizes.
- Circle-shaped cookie cutters in at least two sizes.
- Piping bags and icing nozzles in various sizes.
- Children's rolling pins.

Don't worry if you do not have enough for each child. Part of the learning process for these crafts is about sharing equipment and taking turns.

Setting up and clearing up

The most important thing to remember when setting up is to make the area look both clean and inviting.

If you are planning to tell the Bible story first, it is a good idea to have the craft area out of sight—ideally in a separate room or at least covered with a cloth to make it clear that the area is not to be used just yet. Gather the families together and either read or (better still) tell them the story, then encourage some reflection and discussion on the parts they liked best or what they felt the story meant to them. If appropriate, end with a short prayer before moving to the crafting area.

You may like to provide coffee and tea for the adults while the crafting is taking place. Certainly, if the children eat their crafts straight away, they will want something to drink. Once again, a separate area for this is advisable, or at least a separate table.

To create the crafting area, begin by clearing away as much furniture as possible. The children will need space to craft and the adults will need a good line of sight to see what is going on. Arrange tables and chairs so that there is space for adult helpers as well as children, making sure that the furniture you use can be easily wiped clean. If possible, cover the tables with disposable table cloths or banqueting roll; this makes clearing up much quicker and avoids the hygiene issues that come with working in church buildings.

If there are not enough tables and chairs, cover a large area of floor with tablecloths or banqueting roll and encourage the children to stay seated while they are crafting.

In the middle of the tables, place a supply of antibacterial wipes and a bottle of antibacterial hand cleanser.

Lay the crafting ingredients out on the table before the activity begins; it makes matters much more complicated and dangerous if people are carrying trays and jars around young children. If the food is in danger of becoming too warm or too cold, bring it out at the last minute. Cold icing is very difficult to spread!

Arrange the crafting ingredients so that they can be easily seen, with the same types of ingredients together. Always make a prototype so that the children and their helpers can see what is to be made. If the craft is complicated, you may want to provide two or three examples at different stages of crafting.

Ideally there should be an opportunity for the children to wash their hands before they begin the crafting, but, if this is not possible, the use of antibacterial hand cleanser should be mandatory.

Clearing up is most quickly done by a group of adults while the children are occupied with another activity. However, children can learn much by helping to tidy up, and sharing cleaning tasks can become part of the crafting activity. Do not move tables and chairs while young children are present, however, as the safety issues are too serious.

Resources

● ●

Where to shop

This recipe book has been compiled for busy people who simply do not have the time to wander round markets smelling melons and tasting cheese or to hunt out tiny shops that sell one particular product— even if this is a thoroughly enjoyable thing to do. For this reason, most of the edible ingredients in this book can be purchased in ordinary supermarkets. Some, admittedly, are only stocked in the larger, out-of-town stores, but they can be easily picked up during the course of a weekly family food shop. For those items that might be harder to come by, every effort has been made to offer alternatives.

Ethically aware shoppers will find that the Fairtrade ranges carried by most supermarkets cover most ingredients, except for the decorating items, such as writing icing. Where possible, home-made alternatives have been suggested.

The baking and decorating equipment has, similarly, been kept as simple as possible. However, if you are stocking up for the first time, it might be a good idea either to visit some large craft shops or to look online. Hobbycraft and Lakeland both stock a wide range of cake-making and decorating equipment, which can be bought fairly cheaply, as long as the temptation to add extra interesting things to the list is resisted.

Preparation in advance

Most of the recipes in this book have been used for crafting sessions involving up to 50 children, the oldest of whom is about ten years old and the youngest one year old. With such large numbers and wide age range, I have learnt that it is best to do as much of the preparation in advance as possible. Although parents are encouraged to join in the crafting sessions, those with more than one child cannot watch them all, and it can be quite frustrating

to be struggling to roll out fondant icing, especially if there is a queue for the rolling pin. Equally, some parents of young children may not have encountered cooking crafts before. Every effort should be made to encourage them to craft alongside their children rather than having both parent and child waiting helplessly for help and instruction.

For these reasons, where suggestions have been made for preparation, they have come from hard-earned experience of the capabilities of such a group. If your group is smaller or your children are older, preparation in advance can be put aside. Remember, though, that the craft will take correspondingly longer to complete.

Basic ingredients

All the basic ingredients can be bought at a supermarket. You may have to go to a larger store for the toppings or additional ingredients, but nothing requires a specialist shop.

Savoury crafts

For the bases, you will need:

*   tortillas
*   rice cakes
*   bagels
*   bread rolls
*   rice

The most commonly used toppings are:

*   slices of processed cheese
*   'spaghetti' cheese
*   Parmesan cheese
*   'squirty' cheese
*   vegetables that can be eaten raw, such as carrots, cucumber, peppers and celery
*   black olives
*   mayonnaise, ideally in a bottle

Sweet crafts

You will need the following ingredients for fairy cakes and biscuits:

- plain flour
- self-raising flour
- baking powder
- eggs
- caster sugar
- butter or margarine

You can use the cheapest brand of margarine available, but this can be quite gritty and your cakes may not rise as well. Certainly the biscuits will not taste as good. I tend to use a branded cooking margarine for cakes but prefer the cheapest unsalted butter for biscuits. They are much easier to make with butter, saving you valuable time, and the end result is very tasty.

Toppings

The most commonly used toppings are:

- mini Smarties
- Oreo cookies
- marshmallows, big and small
- edible paper
- digestive biscuits
- syrup pancakes
- icing sugar (if you are going to make your own buttercream icing)

Decorating essentials

Fondant icing

This is the icing most commonly used in the recipes. It is easy to roll out and mould and is not too expensive. You can buy large blocks of white fondant in most supermarkets, and many shops also stock smaller boxes of fondant in five basic colours. Small amounts of different colours can be made using white icing and food colouring. Use only the smallest amount of food colouring: a little goes a long way. It will take a while to knead in so that the colour is spread evenly. If the icing warms up too much in your hands, it will get sticky; if so, just put it in the fridge for five minutes.

For crafts using larger amounts of pink, for example, it is much easier to buy ready-coloured icing from somewhere like Hobbycraft or your local cake decorating shop.

Fondant icing can be rolled out easily, especially if you sandwich it between two pieces of baking parchment while rolling. One way to prevent it sticking is to sprinkle it with icing sugar, but this can make the icing dry out too quickly.

If crafting with children under ten, it is really worth cutting out flat shapes, such as circles to go on top of fairy cakes, beforehand. Sprinkled with icing sugar and kept under clingfilm, they will last a day or two before getting too brittle. Moulding is another matter: the icing can be treated like modelling clay and shaped accordingly.

Fondant icing, once opened, must be stored carefully. Wrap it up in many layers of clingfilm so that it is airtight, or it will be dry and unusable.

Buttercream icing

You can make buttercream icing easily, but be aware that if you use the cheaper sort of margarine to do so, that will be evident in the taste. It really is best to use real, unsalted butter: the cheapest is fine. A quicker alternative is to buy the pots of ready-made buttercream icing that are available in many supermarkets. Once opened, these can be stored in the fridge for quite a long time.

To make buttercream icing, you need to use butter at room temperature, or the process will take much too long. Once your butter is at the right temperature, simply use twice the weight of sifted icing sugar to butter and mix thoroughly. If the icing is too stiff, you can add a drop of water; if too runny, add more icing sugar. Add vanilla or cocoa to make the variations specified in the craft ingredients lists.

Writing icing

You can make writing icing by mixing a small amount of water with icing sugar until you get the consistency you require; then use an icing bag with a fine nozzle. In my experience, this will prove quite messy and difficult to handle for smaller children. By far the best option is to buy little tubes of ready-made writing icing, available from supermarkets and cake decorating shops. The larger tubes are more problematic, as the icing needs to be quite stiff to pipe and the tubes are often too hard to squash for small hands.

Food colourings

It is worth splashing out on the professional food colourings that you can buy in small jars, rather than the bottles of liquid colouring usually found in supermarkets. These have a tendency to make everything runnier and harder to manage. The professional varieties are more solid and, although expensive, last a long time.

Recipes and techniques

Fairy cakes

The simplest and quickest way to provide fairy cakes for a large number of people is probably to go to a large supermarket and buy them! Twelve fairy cakes can cost less than £1 and, if you have no time or equipment for mass production, this is the easiest solution. However, cakes are not difficult to make at home and it only takes about 15 minutes to produce as many as you have oven space to cook. This recipe is practically foolproof and can be multiplied up according to how many cakes you want to make.

Before you begin, it is a good idea to make sure that your oven is level on the floor, otherwise you will produce uneven cakes as the mixture slips to one side in the cooking process. It is also worth working out which way up your oven shelves go: one way is often more level than another. This sounds a bit over-conscientious, but level fairy cakes are easier to decorate.

Ingredients

- 120 g self-raising flour
- 120 g margarine
- 120 g caster sugar
- 2 eggs
- 1 tsp baking powder

These quantities make about 18 small fairy cakes.

1. Turn the oven to 180°C/Gas Mark 4 to pre-heat while you prepare the mixture.
2. Line two fairy cake tins with paper cake cases.
3. Weigh all the ingredients into a large mixing bowl and beat with an electric whisk. You can do this by hand, but it will take a long time and make your arm ache. The mixture will gradually turn a paler colour and become light and fluffy.
4. Check the consistency of the mixture. If you lift a spoonful of it out of the bowl, it should drop off the spoon slowly.
5. Put about a teaspoonful of cake mixture into each paper cake case. Only trial and error will help you discover how much to put in each case. If you want cakes of an equal size, you can pipe the mixture in using an icing bag, but this is time-consuming and not really necessary. After all, once the icing is on, little of the cake will be seen.
6. Place the cakes in the oven for about 8 minutes. This is usually just long enough to wash up your cooking equipment, but if you use a timer you will get a more consistent result. If your oven cooks unevenly, open the door after about 6 minutes and turn the trays round.
7. Check after 8 minutes to see if the cakes look light brown in colour. Test them by pushing down gently with your finger on top of a cake. If it springs back and is firm to the touch, then the cakes are cooked. Here again, trial and error will help you discover how long the cakes need.
8. Once the cakes are cooked, take them out of the tins and let them cool on a wire rack.

Variations

For most crafts, it is best to stick to ordinary fairy cakes, as, once you are familiar with the recipe, they will become very quick and easy to make. However, you could try the following if you want a change.

- Chocolate fairy cakes: swap 20 g cocoa (not drinking chocolate) for 20 g flour.
- Sultana fairy cakes: stir in 20 g sultanas just before the mixture goes in the cases.

Biscuits

These biscuits are very quick and easy to make, as you can use an electric beater rather than crumbling the mixture with your fingers first. Make sure that the butter is at room temperature, though, or it will be very hard work. Once again, you can use margarine instead of butter, but the taste will be poorer. It depends on whether you think people will actually notice what the end product tastes like or whether the joy really lies in the crafting.

Ingredients

- 200 g unsalted butter
- 200 g caster sugar
- 1 beaten egg
- 400 g flour

1. Turn the oven to 180°C/Gas Mark 4 to pre-heat while you prepare the mixture.
2. Beat the sugar and butter together until they lighten in colour and become smooth.
3. Gradually add the egg, beating all the time.
4. Add the flour, beating slowly until the ingredients start to come together into a lump.
5. Bring the dough together into a ball with your hands, then wrap it in clingfilm and put it in the fridge for 10 minutes. Do not be tempted to shortcut this stage, as the chilling process makes the dough much easier to roll out. Similarly, if you make the dough the day before, take it out of the fridge half an hour before you need to roll it or it will crumble.
6. Roll out the dough between two sheets of baking paper. This will stop it sticking to the rolling pin or the work surface and makes rolling much easier.
7. Cut out your shapes and place them on lightly greased baking trays, then put them back in the fridge for another 10 minutes. If you are in a hurry, you can skip this step, but the biscuits cook better from chilled.
8. Cook for about 8 minutes or until light brown. Don't let them get too dark as they will continue cooking on the tray for a few minutes after you have taken them out of the oven.
9. Once the biscuits are cooked, keep them on the tray to harden for a minute or so, then transfer them to a wire rack to cool.

Icing

Much has been written about the techniques of icing and decorating cakes, none of which will be needed for these recipes. All you need is an ordinary kitchen knife for spreading icing. Occasionally a steady hand will be needed—for example, if only part of a cake surface is to be covered in a particular colour (such as the David and Goliath craft on page 49).

Melting chocolate

You can melt chocolate on a stove by breaking it into small pieces and putting it in a bowl over a saucepan of gently simmering water, without allowing the water to touch the bottom of the bowl. Be very careful not to let even a drop of water get into the bowl or the chocolate will become gritty and unusable. It is easier to use a microwave, if you have one: simply break the pieces into a bowl and microwave on medium in 30-second bursts, stopping to stir the chocolate until it is melted.

You cannot melt white chocolate or food colouring. If you want coloured chocolate, you can buy coloured chocolate or candy buttons for melting from Hobbycraft, Lakeland or other cake decorating shops.

Pastry

This book only uses pastry a couple of times—once for the man with leprosy (page 89) and once for the footprints (page 59). For both these recipes, I used a cheese pastry mix. This has the advantage of bubbling up to give a good texture, which is suitable both for cheesy feet and for scruffy men.

Once again you can use margarine instead of butter, but the taste will be poorer. If you use butter, make sure it is at room temperature before you begin.

Ingredients

- 100 g grated cheese (cheddar is probably best, but any hard cheese will do)
- 25 g butter
- 50 g plain flour
- ¼ tsp baking powder

1. Pre-heat the oven to 180°C/Gas Mark 4.
2. Beat all the ingredients together with an electric mixer until they start to come together into a lump. Bring the dough together into a ball with your hands, then wrap it in clingfilm and put it in the fridge for 10 minutes. Do not be tempted to shortcut this stage, as the chilling process makes the dough much easier to roll out. Similarly, if you make the dough the day before, take it out of the fridge half an hour before you need to roll it, or it will crumble.
3. Roll out the dough between two sheets of baking paper. This will stop it sticking to the rolling pin or the work surface and makes rolling much easier.
4. Cut out your pastry shapes and place them on lightly greased baking trays, then put them back into the fridge for another 10 minutes. If you are in a hurry, you can skip this step, but they cook better from chilled.
5. Cook for about 8 minutes or until light brown. Don't let them get too dark as they will continue cooking on the tray for a few minutes after you have taken them out of the oven.
6. Once the pastry shapes are cooked, keep them on the tray to harden for a minute or so, then transfer them to a wire rack to cool.

Gluten- and egg-free cooking

These recipes all work well with gluten-free flour.

The savoury crafts for Jonah (page 51), Daniel (page 54) and 'The sower and the seed' (page 65) all use eggs. For Daniel and 'The sower and the seed', hard cheese cut into appropriate shapes can be used instead. For Jonah, a mini Babybel-style cheese can be substituted: simply cut the cheese in half and use one half as the body of the whale. The other half can then be cut in half again to form the tail. For any of the sweet crafts that include the standard biscuit recipe (page 16), an egg-free gingerbread biscuit can be used. Recipes are available on the internet.

If you wish to make cakes, the egg-free recipe below works well, although the texture of the sponge is denser than when cooked using egg. They do not last as well as ordinary cakes, so ideally they should be eaten the day you cook them.

Ingredients

- 175 g plain flour
- 3 tsp baking powder
- 70 g margarine
- 60 g sugar
- 1 tbsp golden syrup
- 150 ml milk

These quantities make about 18 small fairy cakes.

1. Preheat the oven to 190°C/Gas Mark 5.
2. Line two fairy cake tins with paper cake cases.
3. Beat the margarine, sugar and golden syrup together until lighter in colour and completely mixed in.
4. Combine the flour and baking powder in a bowl.
5. Add about two dessertspoonfuls of flour to the mixed ingredients, then beat again.
6. Add a little milk and mix in.
7. Repeat, alternating flour and milk until all the ingredients are combined.
8. Spoon into paper cake cases and cook for 15–20 minutes, depending on your oven.
9. When golden brown and firm to the touch, remove from the oven. Put on a cake rack to cool.

Edible Bible crafts
Old Testament

Creation

● ●

The story

In the beginning there was nothing. It was dark and empty and shapeless.

'Let there be light!' God said. As soon as he had said the words, light came into existence. God saw that the light was good. God divided the light, so that there was day and there was night.

God made the sky and separated it from the waters below.

God brought the waters together into seas and created dry land.

'Let the land produce plants and trees full of seeds and fruits,' God said. Then all varieties of green and leafy vegetation filled the land, from tall redwood trees to trees bearing olives and oranges, acorns and chestnuts. God saw that all he had made was good.

'Let there be lights in the sky for the night and the day,' God said. 'Let them mark times and seasons, days, months and years.' So the golden sun became the light that shone in the day and the silvery moon the light that beamed in the night sky. God also filled the darkness with stars, and saw that all he had made was good.

'Let the waters be filled with living creatures and the skies with every kind of winged bird. Let them multiply and increase in number.' Then every kind of fish and sea creature swam and splashed in the seas and the air above became filled with colour and shape and sound. There were dolphins and sea horses, eagles, owls, robins and wrens, buzzing bees and beautiful butterflies.

'Let there be all sorts of creatures to move on the land,' God said. So there were sheep and goats, elephants and giraffes, lions, tigers and graceful gazelles.

God looked at everything that he had made and saw that it was good.

Then God made man and woman. He put them in charge of his creation, to care for it and cultivate it for food. God loved the people he had made and he saw that everything he had made was very good. Then God rested.

BIBLE REFERENCE: GENESIS 1:1—2:3, 15

God saw everything that he had made, and indeed, it was very good. And there was evening and there was morning, the sixth day. Thus the heavens and the earth were finished, and all their multitude. (1:31—2:1)

The Lord God took the man and put him in the garden of Eden to till it and keep it. (2:15)

Reflection

What a way to begin a book—with a story that is not only dramatic and action-packed but also seeks to answer some of the 'Why?' and 'How?' questions that children like to ask. The story of creation is beautifully crafted, as each day adds something new to the picture until the perfect whole is achieved, with the chorus of 'and God saw that it was good' emphasising the great gift that has been given to us.

The idea of order being brought out of chaos, of an underlying stability and purpose, is reassuring to children who still find much of their world puzzling, encountering new mysteries each day. In addition, the gradual development of the heavens and earth shows us that while we are an important part of the picture, we must take our place within a wider panorama as the whole of creation sings the praises of God.

Savoury recipe: Creation

Ingredients (per picture)

- One tortilla (use corn tortillas for gluten-free creations)
- One dsp mayonnaise
- Green food colouring
- One slice processed cheese
- Some spaghetti cheese or long strips of cheese (optional)
- Slices of carrot and cucumber
- Pieces of red, yellow and green peppers
- Pieces of tinned sweetcorn

Equipment

- Large circle-shaped cutters
- Small flower-shaped cutters
- Piping bag and medium-sized nozzle (optional)

Preparation

1. Mix the mayonnaise with the food colouring until it looks grass-green.
2. Cut the carrots and cucumber into slices that are roughly 25mm thick.
3. Cut the peppers into pieces that are large enough to fit the flower cutters, but not so large that there is a lot of wastage.
4. You may need to provide vegetable flowers that have already been cut out if the children are very young.
5. Load a piping bag with the green mayonnaise or put it in a dish with a clean paintbrush.

Crafting

1. Lay out the tortilla flat on a plate.
2. Cut out a yellow sun from the cheese slice using the circle-shaped cutter. If you wish, you can add rays using strips of cheese or spaghetti cheese.
3. With the smaller cutter, make flowers out of the vegetable slices and arrange them on the tortilla. Use pieces of sweetcorn for the centre of the flowers.
4. With either a paintbrush or the piping bag, use the green mayonnaise to make stems and leaves for your garden of Eden.

Sweet recipe: Creation

Ingredients (per picture)

- One syrup pancake
- One large Smartie or orange chocolate button (orange 'melts' that are used for making cake coatings are a good size)
- Mini candy-covered chocolate or mini Smarties, or fruit drops if you want to be a bit healthier. Ready-made sugar icing flowers can be used, but these are expensive in large quantities.
- Green writing icing
- Chocolate buttercream icing
- Oreo cookies

Equipment

- Knife for spreading
- Rolling pin and plastic bag

Preparation

Crush the Oreo cookies by placing them in the plastic bag and using the rolling pin to break them up. If you don't mind the mess, older children can do this by themselves. Alternatively, if you don't have enough rolling pins, the cookies can be crumbled in the fingers, but this method is really messy.

Crafting

1. Spread chocolate icing over the bottom third of the pancake.
2. Sprinkle on the crushed Oreo cookies to make the soil.
3. Arrange the mini Smarties into flower shapes, using writing icing to stick them on, or stick on the sugar icing flowers.
4. Draw stems and leaves using the green writing icing.
5. Place the large orange chocolate button at the top of the pancake as the sun.

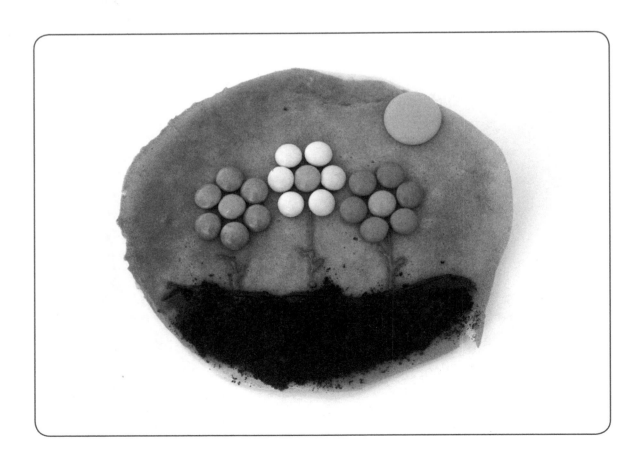

Adam and Eve

The story

One of the creatures in the garden was a snake.

He came to Eve and tempted her.

'Did God really tell you not to eat from any of the trees in the garden?' he asked.

'God told us we can eat from every tree, except the tree in the middle of the garden,' said Eve. 'If we eat from that tree, we will die.'

'You will not die…' said the snake. 'God does not want you to eat from that tree because if you do, you will know right and wrong just as God does.'

Eve looked at the tree. She saw how lovely its fruit looked and thought about what the snake had said. She took some of the fruit and ate it. Then she gave it to Adam and he ate some too.

As soon as they had eaten, Adam and Eve knew what they had done. They realised why God had told them not to eat the fruit. Now they had disobeyed God and it was too late to put things right. They felt guilty and ashamed and when they heard God coming in the garden, they found trees to hide among so he would not see them.

BIBLE REFERENCE: GENESIS 2:18—3:24

So when the woman saw that the tree was good for food, and that it was a delight to the eyes, and that the tree was to be desired to make one wise, she took of its fruit and ate; and she also gave some to her husband, who was with her, and he ate. (3:6)

Reflection

At the heart of this story is our God-given gift of freedom and how we choose to use it. God loves us all deeply and longs for a closer relationship with every one of us. But he wants us to come to him freely, without being pushed or forced to do his will.

We must be obedient to God's way even when he appears to be absent: remember that God only walks in the garden in the evening; the rest of the time Adam and Eve have to trust his word, just as we do. The choices we make, both wise and foolish, affect our lives and the lives of those around us. Adam and Eve chose to disobey God and, by doing so, set themselves apart from him. We too have that choice to make in every action of our lives.

Both the snake and the fruit in the story represent those thoughts and feelings that tempt us into doubting God's purposes for us. The fruit is attractive, as those impulses often are, but should not be trusted.

Reproduced with permission from *Edible Bible Crafts* by Sally Welch, published by Barnabas for Children 2014. www.barnabasinchurches.org.uk

Savoury recipe: The snake

Ingredients (per snake)

- One bagel
- One dsp mayonnaise (ideally in a squirty bottle)
- Slices of carrot, cucumber and red, yellow and green peppers
- One black olive

Equipment

- Knife for cutting

Preparation

Cut the vegetables into slices that are roughly 25mm thick.

For younger children, you may need to cut the bagel into the required shapes beforehand, so that all they need to do is assemble the snake in the correct pattern.

Crafting

1. Slice the bagel in two horizontally, then slice one half in two vertically.
2. Join the two halves to make a snake-like curve (see photograph).
3. Cut part of the second half of the bagel into a point for the snake's tail and a lozenge shape for the head. If the children are old enough to do this for themselves, the shape of the snake's head and tail do not really matter, as long as the body shape is convincing.
4. Decorate by squeezing a wiggly line of mayonnaise along the snake's body. Cut eyes, nostrils and a forked tongue from the vegetable slices and olive.

Reproduced with permission from *Edible Bible Crafts* by Sally Welch, published by Barnabas for Children 2014. www.barnabasinchurches.org.uk

Sweet recipe: The tree

Ingredients (per tree)

- One fairy cake
- One marshmallow
- Buttercream icing
- Green food colouring
- One lolly or cake pop stick
- Mini red candy-covered chocolate or mini Smarties, or fruit drops if you want to be a bit healthier

Equipment

- Knife for spreading

Preparation

Colour the buttercream icing with green food colouring to make the grass and tree green. If you like, you can make two different greens, but this is not strictly necessary.

Crafting

1. Cover the top of the fairy cake with green buttercream icing.
2. Put the lolly stick firmly into the marshmallow.
3. With the knife, spread the buttercream on to the marshmallow. You can make the buttercream runnier and dip the marshmallow into it, but this probably requires more skill.
4. Push the 'tree' firmly into the fairy cake. Decorate with 'apples'.

Reproduced with permission from *Edible Bible Crafts* by Sally Welch, published by Barnabas for Children 2014. www.barnabasinchurches.org.uk

Noah

● ●

The story

Many years passed and the land became full of people. But few remembered who God was… God knew that the world had become an evil place, full of greed, hatred and violence. He decided to wash it clean and start all over again.

There was one man who remembered God. His name was Noah. Noah had a wife and three sons, Shem, Ham and Japheth.

'Noah!' God said one day. '… I want you to build an ark—a huge boat that will float on the flood waters that I will send to wash the earth clean…'

Noah set about building the ark… It took him many years of his life, and the people around him watched and thought he was mad.

The ark was ready. God told Noah to collect two of every kind of living creature… The animals came to Noah as if they too knew what God had planned, and Noah took them all on board the ark. Then God shut the door.

Outside the rain began to fall… Everything that lived upon the earth was destroyed by the flood. But the ark that God had told Noah to build floated on the waters…

Days passed. Weeks passed, and still the rain fell down.

Then one day it stopped. The ark floated gently.

Slowly, very slowly, the waters began to go down… But Noah waited until God told him it was time to leave the ark.

Then they came out, Noah, his family and all the creatures that had been kept safe… Noah thanked God for keeping them all safe.

'I will never destroy all the earth with water again,' promised God. 'I have put a rainbow in the sky, as a sign of my promise.'

BIBLE REFERENCE: GENESIS 6:11—9:16 (ABRIDGED)

'I have set my bow in the clouds, and it shall be a sign of the covenant between me and the earth. When I bring clouds over the earth and the bow is seen in the clouds, I will remember my covenant that is between me and you and every living creature of all flesh; and the waters shall never again become a flood to destroy all flesh.' (9:13–15)

Reflection

The story of Noah is a story of mercy and rescue, and of the unfailing relationship between God and his children. Although we live in a fallen, broken world, and although we have brought much of the distress and sorrow that surrounds us upon ourselves, God is still seeking to draw us closer to him. Natural and human catastrophes might mask God's love from us, but Noah has been kept safe in the ark and now lives in security under the rainbow, a sign of grace and hope for all people. God has not abandoned the world that he has made, and he never will.

The monkey's cheerful face reminds us that, once again, all of creation is involved in this story, for God's will carries the promise of a restored creation and a 'new heaven and a new earth'.

Savoury recipe: The rainbow

Ingredients (per rainbow)

- One bagel
- 50 g rice cooked in water with blue food colouring added to it. (Blue food is very difficult to find, but if you do find any, use that in preference to dyeing the rice)
- 50 g each of carrot and red cabbage
- 50 g each of tomato, red pepper and green pepper
- Margarine, butter, mayonnaise or squirty cheese to spread

Equipment

- Knife for spreading

Preparation

Grate the carrot and red cabbage. Finely chop the tomato and peppers.

Crafting

1. Slice the bagel in two horizontally, then slice one half in two vertically.
2. Spread the bagel with margarine, butter or cheese. The spread needs to be quite thick as it provides the 'glue' for the rest of the food.
3. Carefully place the different foods on the bagel in rainbow order. For young children, this may be too delicate a task. In this case, simply sprinkling on different coloured foods for a rainbow effect will be fine.

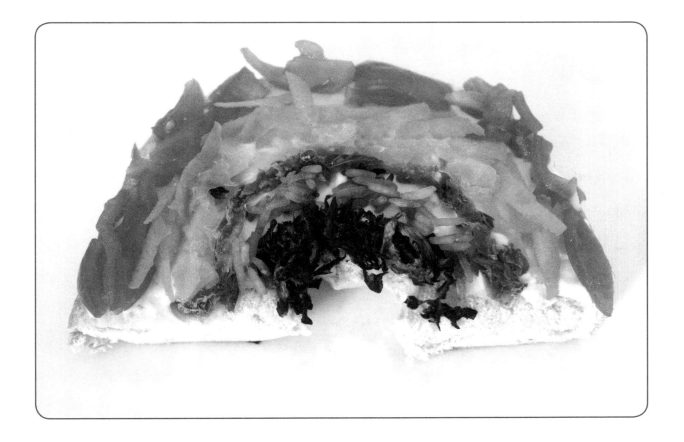

Reproduced with permission from *Edible Bible Crafts* by Sally Welch, published by Barnabas for Children 2014. www.barnabasinchurches.org.uk

Sweet recipe: Noah's monkey

Ingredients (per monkey)

- One fairy cake
- Two Cheerios
- Chocolate buttercream icing
- Chocolate sprinkles
- One strawberry lace
- Chocolate writing icing
- Two mini chocolate buttons or chocolate drops
- Pink fondant icing

Equipment

- Knife for spreading
- Rolling pin

Preparation

Roll out the pink fondant icing to about 4mm thick and cut out a face shape. Since rolling out fondant icing is quite difficult, it is better to do this beforehand, sprinkling the faces with icing sugar to stop them sticking together.

Place the chocolate sprinkles in a shallow dish or saucer.

Crafting

1. Cover the top of the fairy cake with chocolate buttercream icing.
2. Dip the top of the fairy cake in the dish of sprinkles so that they stick to the icing.
3. Add a Cheerio on either side of the fairy cake, for ears.
4. Place the fondant face on to the fairy cake.
5. Add chocolate drop eyes and writing icing nostrils.
6. Use a piece of the strawberry lace to make a cheerful grin.

It is possible to use two sprinkles as eyebrows, but this is quite fiddly and should be omitted for younger children.

Jacob

● ●

The story

Jacob saw some shepherds and their sheep waiting by a large well. He approached them and asked where they were from.

'We are from Haran,' they replied.

Jacob was delighted. That was where his uncle lived.

'Do you know Laban?' he asked hopefully.

'Yes,' they replied. 'That's Laban's daughter, Rachel, over there,' said the shepherds.

Jacob looked up. He saw a shepherdess leading her flock of sheep towards the well. Jacob went to meet Rachel and watered her sheep from the well. Then he kissed her and told her that he was her cousin. She was so pleased, she ran to tell her father.

Laban… took Jacob home and made him welcome as part of the family.

After Jacob had stayed a month, Laban asked Jacob how he should be paid for working for his uncle…

Jacob thought carefully. He had only been with Laban a short time, but he had fallen in love with Laban's youngest daughter, Rachel.

'I will work for you for seven years, if you let me marry Rachel,' said Jacob.

Laban agreed… At the end of the seven years, Laban organised a big feast to celebrate his daughter's marriage. But Laban intended to trick Jacob… Instead of marrying Rachel, Jacob married Leah, Laban's eldest daughter.

When Jacob found out, it was too late.

'Why did you trick me?' asked Jacob angrily. He wanted Rachel, not Leah.

'It is our custom,' replied Laban. 'But I will let you marry Rachel now and have both daughters, if you agree to work for me for another seven years.'

Jacob agreed. He loved Rachel very much.

BIBLE REFERENCE: GENESIS 29:1–20

Jacob loved Rachel; so he said, 'I will serve you seven years for your younger daughter Rachel.' Laban said, 'It is better that I give her to you than that I should give her to any other man; stay with me.' So Jacob served seven years for Rachel, and they seemed to him but a few days because of the love he had for her. (vv. 18–20)

Reflection

The story of Jacob and Rachel is that of patient love, of Jacob's willingness to see the bigger picture and to wait for what he wants. Having tricked his brother Esau out of his birthright, Jacob has to leave his own land, in fear for his life.

Confident that God is directing his steps, Jacob journeys towards the land of his kinsmen. Jacob arrives at the well that is used by all the herdsmen for their sheep. While he is there, Rachel arrives with her father's flock of sheep, for she is in charge of them. Jacob falls instantly in love with Rachel, and the first demonstration of this love is a practical one: he helps her to water the sheep.

The love of Jacob for Rachel is so great that he is prepared to work for Rachel's father for seven years so that he might marry her. The time passes quickly for him, because his love is so deep and enduring. But then Laban plays a cruel trick on Jacob, and on Rachel as well, for what must she have thought when she discovered that her older sister was married to the man she loved? Perhaps it was a fitting punishment for a man who had, after all, played similar tricks on his own father and brother. But in the end his patience triumphs and Rachel and he can become husband and wife.

Reproduced with permission from *Edible Bible Crafts* by Sally Welch, published by Barnabas for Children 2014. www.barnabasinchurches.org.uk

Savoury recipe: Jacob's well

Ingredients (per well)

- One tortilla
- One small brown bread roll
- One stick of celery
- One piece of carrot
- Squirty cheese (optional)

Equipment

- Knife for cutting
- Circular cutters
- Metal skewer (optional)

Preparation

The preparation for this craft really depends on the age of the children. For young children, you might have to cut out the well from the bread roll, cut the celery into sticks and cut a square piece of tortilla. Older children can do all these things by themselves.

The carrot 'bucket' is an extra touch that will be quite challenging but is fun to try.

Crafting

1. Cut out a circle from the centre of the brown bread roll. If you want an authentic 'roughened' look to the outside of the well, cut off the crust with a larger circular cutter.
2. Cut two sticks of celery for the roof support and push them firmly into the roll. This may be harder than it looks: you might need to make a hole first with a skewer.
3. Cut a square from the tortilla, fold it in half and position over the two celery sticks. You can use squirty cheese to help glue the tortilla roof in position, but otherwise just balance it carefully.
4. Cut a 3cm length of carrot, ideally where the carrot gets wider. Hollow out the wider end carefully to make the bucket shape.
5. For the handle of the bucket, cut a thin slice of carrot, then cut it in half and cut out a semi-circular handle.
6. Make two holes in the rim of the bucket using a skewer, then insert the carrot handle into the holes.

Reproduced with permission from *Edible Bible Crafts* by Sally Welch, published by Barnabas for Children 2014. www.barnabasinchurches.org.uk

Sweet recipe: Jacob's well

Ingredients (per well)

- One fairy cake
- Two chocolate-covered biscuit sticks (Mikado biscuits are especially good)
- One piece of rice paper
- White fondant icing
- Black, grey or terracotta food colouring
- Writing icing

Equipment

- Small circular cutter

Preparation

Depending on what colour you are going to make your bucket or jar for water, mix the fondant icing with the food colouring until you get the shade you require.

Crafting

1. Cut a hole in the centre of the fairy cake using the small cutter. Insert the biscuit sticks into the fairy cake, one on each side of the hole.
2. Cut a square of rice paper and gently crease it down the middle. Balance the rice paper on top of the biscuit stick supports. You can use writing icing to stick the paper to the biscuit sticks or simply balance it on top.
3. Make a bucket or jar shape from the fondant icing and place it on top of the fairy cake well.

Joseph

The story

Jacob now had twelve sons, but he loved Joseph more than his other children, and Joseph knew it...

Jacob gave Joseph a very special long-sleeved coat. When Joseph's brothers saw it, they knew that he was loved much more than they were. They hated him...

Joseph's brothers had taken the sheep to graze. His father sent Joseph to find out how they were...

As soon as Joseph reached them, the brothers tore off his coat and forced him down into the well. They were sitting eating a meal when they saw some Midianite traders, loaded up with spices, on their way to Egypt. It was not long before Judah had suggested a plan to sell their brother...

His brothers then killed a goat and dipped Joseph's fine coat in the blood. They returned to their father and said they had found it.

Jacob believed that his much-loved son had been attacked by a wild animal and was dead. He was overcome with grief.

BIBLE REFERENCE: GENESIS 37:3–34

> Now Israel loved Joseph more than any other of his children, because he was the son of his old age; and he had made him a long robe with sleeves. But when his brothers saw that their father loved him more than all his brothers, they hated him, and could not speak peaceably to him. (vv. 3–4)

Reflection

There can be few people who do not know the story of Joseph, thanks largely to the famous musical by Andrew Lloyd Webber, which has shaped our impressions of the story into one of colour and dancing. However, at the root of the tale is a reminder of the dangers of envy and jealousy, both for those who suffer from them and those who feed them, however inadvertently.

Joseph was Jacob's favourite son, which perhaps he could not have avoided: 'he was the son of his old age', as the Bible story says. But Jacob should not have demonstrated this favouritism before his other sons, who grew to resent Joseph in all his finery. Driven by these corrosive emotions, Joseph's brothers committed the atrocious act of plotting to kill him and to destroy their father's happiness by so doing.

We know that Reuben's remorse for this deed was great, and Jacob's sorrow almost killed him. How unhappy must that family have been in the years after Joseph's disappearance! But once again, we are shown that God can work for the good in all circumstances, for it was precisely because Joseph was in Egypt that he could be the means by which his family was later saved from starvation.

Joseph's faithfulness to God in all the ups and downs of his life, his steadfastness and loyalty even when thrown into prison for years, was rewarded as he was finally able to restore his family to wholeness. They had learnt their lesson—none of them was prepared to lose another brother—and Joseph had learnt his, too, for his arrogance before his brothers had melted in his joy at being reunited with them once again.

Savoury recipe: Joseph's coat

Ingredients (per coat)

- One tortilla
- Tomato ketchup
- Mayonnaise
- Squirty cheese
- Tomato, peppers and cucumber to decorate (optional)

Equipment

- Knife for cutting
- Piping bags

Preparation

Younger children may need a cardboard template in the shape of a coat to help them with cutting the tortilla.

Put small quantities of the cheese, ketchup and mayonnaise in different piping bags. The disposable bags are easiest to use: you don't need a piping nozzle, just snip the end of the bag after you have filled it. If the ketchup is too runny to pipe properly, you can add a bit of flour or cornflour to thicken it, but this will lighten the colour.

Crafting

1. Cut out the shape of a long coat from the tortilla, using a template if you have one.
2. Carefully pipe patterns on to the tortilla coat using the different sauces.
3. If you like, you can cut shapes out of tomatoes, peppers and cucumber to decorate the coat further. The Bible does not say how the coat was decorated, after all.

Sweet recipe: Joseph's coat

Ingredients (per coat)

- One syrup pancake
- A selection of fruit

Equipment

- Knife for cutting

Preparation

You may want to provide a template for the coat shape.

Crafting

1. Cut the syrup pancake into the shape of a coat.
2. Slice the fruit so that one side of each piece is flat. Place the fruit in patterns on to the pancake coat.

Reproduced with permission from *Edible Bible Crafts* by Sally Welch, published by Barnabas for Children 2014. www.barnabasinchurches.org.uk

Baby Moses

The story

Joseph lived to see his own great-great-grand-children. Before his death, he told his brothers that God would one day take them back to the Promised Land…

Years passed and Joseph's descendants were very many in the land of Egypt. A time came when the new Pharaoh looked at the Isarelites who lived in the land, and he was afraid.

'There are too many Israelites,' he said. 'Soon they will join with our enemies and overcome us. We must enslave them and make them build us new cities.'

So the Egyptians oppressed the Israelites. They made them work hard for them and ill treated them. But still the Israelites seemed to grow in number and God blessed them.

Then Pharaoh ordered the midwives to kill all baby boys born to the Israelite women. The midwives would not obey Pharaoh; they told him that the women were strong and gave birth before they arrived to help… But Pharaoh had another plan. He gave an order that all baby boys must be thrown into the River Nile and drowned.

One day an Israelite woman gave birth to a son. She hid him until he was three months old. She could not let the Egyptians take her baby away.

Then, when he was too big to hide any longer, she put the baby in a basket. She coated it with tar to make it waterproof, and hid it in the reeds along the bank of the River Nile.

When the Pharaoh's daughter came to bathe in the river, she heard the sound of a baby crying and felt sorry for him.

'Shall I find someone to nurse him for you?' asked Miriam, who was watching nearby.

'Yes,' said the princess. 'I will keep this baby and call him Moses.'

Miriam went to fetch her mother.

'Look after this baby until he is old enough to live with me,' said the princess. Miriam's mother took her little son away to care for him.

BIBLE REFERENCE: EXODUS 1:8—2:9

> Then his sister said to Pharaoh's daughter, 'Shall I go and get you a nurse from the Hebrew women to nurse the child for you?' Pharaoh's daughter said to her, 'Yes.' So the girl went and called the child's mother. Pharaoh's daughter said to her, 'Take this child and nurse it for me, and I will give you your wages.' So the woman took the child and nursed it. (2:7–9)

Reflection

Miriam was Moses' big sister and the part she plays in the story of the children of Israel is often overlooked. How must she have felt as she stood watching to see what happened to her baby brother? How her heart must have leapt in fear when she saw no less a personage than the Pharaoh's daughter open his basket! How great her joy when she realised that not only would her brother survive but that he could become part of their family again as her mother nursed him.

This story is wonderful for teaching children about sibling relationships and responsibility, and encouraging them to empathise with both helpless younger brother and watchful big sister.

Reproduced with permission from *Edible Bible Crafts* by Sally Welch, published by Barnabas for Children 2014. www.barnabasinchurches.org.uk

Savoury recipe: Baby Moses

Ingredients (per baby)

- One small bridge roll
- One slice of ham
- One slice of cheese, about 5mm thick
- One black olive
- Small piece of red pepper or tomato

Equipment

- Knife for cutting
- Small circular cutter
- Icing nozzle (optional)

Preparation

Slice the bridge roll in half, scoop out some of the bread and place it to one side. If the children are very young, cut out eyes from the olive and a smile from the tomato or red pepper. (The end of a circular icing nozzle is very good for making round eyes.)

Crafting

1. With the bread that has been scooped out of the roll, mould an oval body shape and place it in one half of the roll.
2. Cut out a circle of cheese, using the cutter.
3. Put the cheese at one end of the roll and cover the bread body with a ham blanket. Position pieces of olive for eyes and tomato or red pepper for a mouth.

Sweet recipe: Baby Moses

Ingredients (per baby)

- One paper cake case
- One Shredded Wheat
- Milk chocolate
- White fondant icing
- Pink food colouring or pink fondant icing
- Black writing icing

Equipment

- Spoon

Preparation

Make a small amount of pink fondant icing, using white icing and colouring.

Break the chocolate into small pieces in a mixing bowl and melt, either in the microwave or by placing the bowl over simmering water and stirring gently until the chocolate melts. This needs to be done just before the craft session, especially if the building is cold, as the chocolate will solidify quite quickly.

Crafting

1. Crush the Shredded Wheat and mix it with the melted chocolate, until the Shredded Wheat is completely covered with chocolate.
2. While the chocolate is still melted, place a spoonful of the mixture in the paper cake case and hollow out the centre.
3. While the mixture is setting, make an oval 'baby in a blanket' shape from the white fondant icing. Add a pink face, and use the black writing icing for the features. Place the baby in the basket.

Moses and the Red Sea

The story

Together, Moses and Aaron went to see Pharaoh.

'We have come with a message from the Lord, the God of Israel: "Let my people go, so that they can worship me,"' they said…

When Pharaoh refused, God sent plagues of gnats, flies and locusts; every Egyptian animal died, and the people were covered in boils; violent hailstorms battered the land, and the whole of Egypt was plunged into darkness…

Then God told Moses that this time the firstborn of every living creature in Egypt would die—including Pharaoh's own son. But God would protect his people and keep them safe…

That night, after midnight, every firstborn Egyptian died…

Pharaoh called Moses and Aaron and told them to go. 'Take your cattle and sheep and leave this land!' he shouted. The Egyptians gave the Israelites gold and silver—all they asked for.

Then Moses told the people that God would lead them to Canaan. By day God appeared to the people as a pillar of cloud leading them, and by night God was a pillar of fire. God did not take them by the road that crossed the land of the Philistines but by the desert road towards the Red Sea.

It was not long before Pharaoh began to regret that he had let his workforce of slaves leave Egypt. He decided to pursue them and bring them back…

The Israelites soon saw that they were coming after them and were terrified…

But Moses was not afraid. He knew that God would save his people.

The pillar of cloud moved behind the people so it stood between them and the Egyptians and brought confusion to Pharaoh's men.

Then Moses stretched out his hand over the Red Sea and God sent a wind to blow back the waters through the night so that all the Israelites could pass over safely to the other side on dry land.

The Egyptians started to follow, but Moses stretched out his hand again, now from the safety of the far bank, and God sent the water to cover Pharaoh and his army and chariots in the Red Sea. None of the Egyptians survived; but all God's people were safe.

BIBLE REFERENCE: EXODUS 8:16—12:36; 13:17—14:29

> Then Moses stretched out his hand over the sea. The Lord drove the sea back by a strong east wind all night, and turned the sea into dry land; and the waters were divided. (14:21)

Reflection

It must have seemed like the last straw to Moses and his people. Despite the unwillingness of Pharaoh, finally Moses was allowed to take the Israelites out of Egypt. But even that was not enough, for Pharaoh changed his mind and his army came after them.

The Israelites were halted by the waters of the Red Sea; it seemed as if their brief moment of freedom had come to an end. But Moses knew better. He alone of all the people continued to have faith in a rescuer God: 'Do not be afraid, stand firm,' he told his people (Exodus 14:13), and the seas were parted in a way that would be told and retold throughout the history of the children of Israel.

Sometimes it seems that one disaster follows another, that there is no end to it. Then is the time to remember God's promise that we will be his children and he will care for us. But consider, too, that this was only the beginning of the trials of the Israelites. It would be many years before they reached the promised land, and their faith would be tested many times on the journey.

Reproduced with permission from *Edible Bible Crafts* by Sally Welch, published by Barnabas for Children 2014. www.barnabasinchurches.org.uk

We too must learn to trust in God's timing and learn to accept that his ways are not our ways. Sometimes our prayers will be answered as we hope and expect; at others, it may be many years before we feel that our patience has been rewarded and our prayers answered. But we must always believe that God has our best interests at heart and his plan for us is the right one.

Savoury recipe: The Red Sea

Ingredients (per Red Sea)

- One portion of cooked rice, boiled in water to which blue food colouring has been added
- Two tsp Parmesan cheese or other finely grated cheese (a cheaper alternative to cheese for large quantities is cheese biscuits, crumbled)
- One carrot
- One thick slice of cucumber

Equipment

- One plastic jelly pot or bowl per person (disposable clear plastic bowls are best, as the children can see through them)
- Knife for cutting
- Plastic bag and rolling pin for crushing biscuits (if that option is chosen)

Preparation

If the children are very young, you might want to carve some of the carrot and cucumber into fish shapes. Otherwise, simply cut the carrot and cucumber pieces about 3 mm thick.

Crafting

1. Carefully pile the blue rice on either side of the bowl, leaving a space between the two piles.
2. Sprinkle the finely grated cheese or crushed cheese biscuits on the central gap. This will be the dry sand that the Israelites walked across.
3. Carve fish and other sea creatures out of the carrot and cucumber and add them to the blue sea.

39

Reproduced with permission from *Edible Bible Crafts* by Sally Welch, published by Barnabas for Children 2014. www.barnabasinchurches.org.uk

Sweet recipe: The Red Sea

Ingredients (per sea)

- One portion of blue jelly (if you cannot find any in the shops, make up some lemon jelly and add blue food colouring to the boiling water)
- One digestive biscuit
- Orange fondant icing

Equipment

- One plastic jelly pot or bowl per person (disposable clear plastic bowls are best, as the children can see through them)
- Plastic bag and rolling pin for crushing biscuit

Preparation

None, unless you need to make blue jelly.

Crafting

1. Roughly chop the jelly so that it looks like wave shapes. Place it carefully in the plastic bowl, on either side.
2. Place the digestive biscuit in a plastic food bag and crush it with the rolling pin. Put the crumbs in the central space between the waves.
3. Using the orange fondant icing, make fish shapes to swim in the jelly sea.

Gideon

The story

Gideon, the son of Joash, was trying to thresh wheat in secret, out of sight of the Midianites.

An angel came to sit under an oak tree and watched him.

'God is with you, mighty warrior!' the angel said to Gideon.

'Then why are we in so much trouble?' Gideon answered. 'God brought our ancestors out of Egypt only to let us die under the Midianites!'

'You can change that,' said the angel. 'God wants you to save Israel from the Midianites.'

'But why would God send me? I am no one! I belong to the smallest clan in my tribe; I am the least in my family!'

'You can do this because I will be with you,' said the angel. 'We will save Israel together.'…

The Israelite army gathered together and made camp.

'You have too many soldiers,' said God to Gideon. 'When the battle is won, the people will say that they did it in their own strength.'…

Gideon obeyed God. He now had an army of just 300 men to fight the Midianites.

'It is time!' said God to Gideon during the night. 'Now you will defeat your enemies!'…

Gideon divided the men into three groups, and gave each man a trumpet and a burning torch covered by an empty jar. In the darkness, the Israelites surrounded the enemy camp. At Gideon's signal, he and his men blew their trumpets and smashed the jars.

'For the Lord and for Gideon!' they cried.

The Midianites and the Amalekites were terrified. They stumbled and fell upon each other in the darkness. They killed each other with their swords. Those who remained fled to the hills.

It was just as God had said. God had rescued the Israelites once again.

BIBLE REFERENCE: JUDGES 6:11–16; 7:2–22

> Then the Lord turned to him and said, 'Go in this might of yours and deliver Israel from the hand of Midian; I hereby commission you.' He responded, 'But sir, how can I deliver Israel? My clan is the weakest in Manasseh, and I am the least in my family.' (6:14–15)

Reflection

It is not always the bravest, the strongest or the most obvious person who gets chosen by God to do his work. Gideon knew only too well how unfit he was to be a hero: even God had to work hard to persuade him that he alone could carry out God's plan to save Israel. Finally convinced, Gideon was sent into battle with a comically small number of troops. How frightened he must have been as he stood in the dark, with his pitiful trick of hidden torches, and how wonderful was the might of God who set the Midianites fighting among themselves in the confusion!

The story of Gideon shows us that sometimes it is the weakest individual who can show God's strength and power most clearly, if we only allow God to work through us.

Reproduced with permission from *Edible Bible Crafts* by Sally Welch, published by Barnabas for Children 2014. www.barnabasinchurches.org.uk

Savoury recipe: Gideon's jar

Ingredients (per jar)

- One section of cucumber (at least 5 cm)
- Squirty cheese, mustard and tomato ketchup, as available

Equipment

- Knife for cutting (or pumpkin carving tools if you can get hold of them)

Preparation

If the children are very young, you might want to hollow out the cucumber for them, to make the interior of the jar.

Crafting

1. Using knives and other carving tools, make patterns on the outside of the cucumber jar.
2. Decorate with squirty cheese, mustard and so on.

Sweet recipe: Gideon's jar

Ingredients (per jar)

- One ice cream cone with a flat bottom
- Writing icing, cake decorations and so on

Equipment

- None

Preparation

None.

Crafting

Decorate the cone as preferred, using whatever is available. Stick on any decorations with writing icing, or just use the writing icing to make patterns on the cone.

Jericho

● ●

The story

Joshua camped with the people outside Jericho. They celebrated the Passover and waited until God told them what to do next.

Then a man with a sword in his hand appeared in Joshua's path. Joshua knew he had been sent by God, and fell to his knees.

'I am the commander of God's army,' said the man. 'This is what you must do. Seven priests must lead you in a march around the city walls. The priests must walk in front of the ark, each carrying a trumpet, for six days. On the seventh day, they must march around the city walls seven times, blowing their trumpets. On the long trumpet blast, signal to the people to shout. Then the city walls will collapse.'

The gates of the city of Jericho stood before Joshua and his army, firmly closed against them.

For six days they marched as God had told them. On the seventh day, at the sound of the long trumpet blast, the people shouted, and the walls of Jericho crumbled and fell down.

Then the Israelites marched into the city. God had given them the victory.

BIBLE REFERENCE: JOSHUA 5:10—6:21

> The Lord said to Joshua, 'See, I have handed Jericho over to you, along with its king and soldiers.' (6:2)

Reflection

The fall of Jericho is one of the best-known Old Testament stories and is packed full of drama and action. What could be more exciting than the walls of a city crashing to the ground, sending shock waves through the entire countryside? Yet at its very heart is perceived inaction, for Joshua does not defeat the Canaanites by fighting but by prayer. At the front of the procession, which does no more than march round the city, are seven priests and the ark of the covenant. All that is needed to succeed in this battle is the symbol of the promise God made to his people that he would care for them.

Once again we are reminded that great things can be done through us by God, in his name. All we need is the faith to put aside our own wants and needs and listen to what he is asking us to do.

Reproduced with permission from *Edible Bible Crafts* by Sally Welch, published by Barnabas for Children 2014. www.barnabasinchurches.org.uk

Savoury recipe: Jericho's wall

Ingredients (per wall)

- One tortilla
- One slice of bread
- One piece of cheese
- One carrot
- Three slices of salami or similar
- One stick of celery

Equipment

- Knife for cutting
- Small circular cutter

Preparation

If the children are very young, you might need to chop the salami into oblong shapes and slice the carrot into thin sticks, about 4 cm long.

Crafting

1. Cut the crusts off the bread to make a long rectangle, just smaller than the tortilla. Place in the middle of the tortilla. This is the wall.
2. To make the bricks, arrange oblongs of salami in alternate lines to make a brick pattern.
3. Cut out a circle of cheese to form the sun, and arrange the sticks of carrot around it for the rays.
4. Slice the celery stick thinly and arrange beneath the bread wall so that it looks like grass.

Sweet recipe: Jericho's wall

Ingredients (per wall)

- One piece of sponge cake, cooked in a rectangular tin to a depth of 15–20 mm
- Buttercream icing

Equipment

- Knife for cutting and spreading

Preparation

None.

Crafting

1. Cut the sponge cake into brick shapes.
2. Build the bricks into a wall, using buttercream icing as cement.

Reproduced with permission from *Edible Bible Crafts* by Sally Welch, published by Barnabas for Children 2014. www.barnabasinchurches.org.uk

David and Goliath

The story

The Israelite battle line was gathered on one hill; the Philistines were on the other. In between them was a valley, and in the valley was the Philistine champion, a giant of a man named Goliath.

His huge head was protected by a bronze helmet; his huge body by bronze armour; his muscular legs were protected by bronze greaves and he carried a bronze javelin on his back. In his hand was a spear with a heavy iron point. Day by day, Goliath walked up and down in front of the Israelites, challenging them to send a man to fight him.

The Israelites were terrified. No one would go.

One day David brought food supplies to the Israelite camp. He saw Goliath walking up and down and shouting, and he saw that no one stood up to him.

'How dare he challenge us!' said David to the men around him. 'We have the living God on our side.'

King Saul heard the rumours among his soldiers and sent for David.

'Our army should not be afraid of this warrior,' David said. 'I will go out and fight him.'

'This giant is a professional fighter,' Saul said. 'You are just a boy.'

'I look after my father's sheep,' answered David, 'and have to fight off lions and bears to protect them. If God can save me from the paw of the lion and bear, he can surely save me from this Philistine.'

David tried the king's armour but it was too big and heavy for him. Instead he took his sling and chose five small stones from the stream.

When Goliath saw him, he sneered. David shouted back.

'You have sword and spear and javelin but I have the living God on my side! Today the whole world will know that there is a God in Israel who can save us.'

David slipped a stone into his sling and whirled it around his head. The stone shot through the air and hit Goliath's forehead. He sank to the ground and the Israelite army cheered. Their enemy's champion was dead and his army had run away.

BIBLE REFERENCE: 1 SAMUEL 17:1–51

'All this assembly may know that the Lord does not save by sword and spear; for the battle is the Lord's and he will give you into our hand.' (v. 47)

Reflection

In our lives there will be events that are so big and so frightening that they fill our thoughts, taking up all our energy and attention. Some of these horrors will be real, some will be imaginary and some will turn out not to be horrors after all, just events that, after all the dread and the anticipation, were quite harmless.

David defeated his giant, Goliath, not with conventional weapons or vast amounts of resource but with his own courage and a firm belief in God. Sometimes the bravest people are not the biggest or the strongest but those who are not afraid to be who they are and to trust God for the rest. With five small stones, David could do nothing; with five small stones and God, he saved his people.

Reproduced with permission from *Edible Bible Crafts* by Sally Welch, published by Barnabas for Children 2014. www.barnabasinchurches.org.uk

Savoury recipe: David

Ingredients (per David)

- One large flatbread cracker. If you cannot find a cracker big enough, a pitta bread would be a good substitute
- One green pepper
- One carrot
- One small round wax-coated cheese (such as Babybel)
- One piece of celery
- One piece of red pepper

Equipment

- Knife for cutting

Preparation

Peel the carrot and cut into thin sticks. If the children are very young, you might need to shape the body out of the green pepper and even make the 'hair'.

Crafting

1. Shape a body out of the green pepper and place it in the middle of the cracker.
2. Cut sticks of carrot for arms and legs.
3. Make a belt from a thin slice of celery.
4. Take the wax coating off the cheese. Carefully cut a serrated edge along one half of the wax coating so that it looks like a fringe. Put the coating back on the cheese.
5. Use small pieces of green and red pepper for eyes and a smile.

Sweet recipe: Goliath

Ingredients (per giant)

- One fairy cake
- Vanilla buttercream icing
- Red food colouring
- Chocolate buttercream icing
- Chocolate sprinkles
- Two chocolate drops
- Piece of strawberry lace

Equipment

- Knife for cutting and spreading

Preparation

Mix the vanilla buttercream icing and food colouring together to create a skin colour.

Crafting

1. Spread the pink icing over the central section of the fairy cake, and the chocolate icing over the top and bottom. If this is too complicated, the cake can be all pink.
2. Carefully cover the top and bottom of the cake with chocolate sprinkles to make hair and a beard.
3. Use two chocolate drops to form the eyes, and some strawberry lace to make a downturned mouth. You can add two sprinkles for frowning eyebrows if you wish, but this is quite tricky.

49

Jonah

● ●

The story

The Assyrians were a growing threat to God's people… So when God called on Jonah, one of his prophets, to go to Nineveh and warn them to repent of their wickedness, he was not happy…

Jonah was so unhappy that he went to the port of Joppa to look for a ship going to Tarshish, about as far in the opposite direction as he could go…

The ship had not long been out to sea when the wind grew stronger and a violent storm arose…

The men prayed to their gods and threw their cargo over the side to lighten the ship…

Then the captain noticed that Jonah was missing. He went below deck to find him…

'What terrible thing have you done that your God is punishing us?' the sailors asked Jonah. 'Who are you?'

'I worship the God who made the land and the sea,' Jonah replied. 'But I have run away from him. This is all my fault. There is only one thing you can do: you must throw me overboard.'

The sailors listened in horror. They did not want to kill Jonah; but they did not want to die either…

Then the sailors prayed to the living God. 'Do not blame us for taking this man's life! We can do nothing else!' They picked up Jonah and threw him over the side.

The wind dropped straight away; the waves grew calm. The sailors were amazed and fell to their knees. They had seen the power of the living God.

Jonah, meanwhile, had sunk beneath the waves and felt himself falling down, down, down and strangled by seaweed. Then, as he felt his life draining away from him, he called to God for help. And God answered.

God sent a huge fish to swallow him whole— and saved him.

Jonah stayed inside the body of the fish for three days and three nights. He thought about what had happened and how he had tried to run away from God. He remembered that he had once promised to serve God and do whatever he asked. Then he praised God and promised to serve him again because only his God had the power to save.

Then God spoke to the huge fish and commanded it to spit Jonah out on to dry land.

BIBLE REFERENCE: JONAH 1—2

> 'But I with the voice of thanksgiving will sacrifice to you; what I have vowed I will pay. Deliverance belongs to the Lord!' (2:9)

Reflection

The book of Jonah begins with the tale of Jonah's disobedience towards God. It is quite simple: God asks him to tell the people of Nineveh that they must repent of their wickedness. This is Jonah's job; he is a prophet, after all. But Jonah is frightened, and the ensuing disasters that happen to him and the people around him are a direct consequence of his fear.

However, God does not give up on Jonah; he does not turn away in disgust and find another prophet to carry out the task. Instead he leads Jonah to the realisation of the importance of his role and his acceptance of it.

Ironically, Jonah then became angry about the success of his preaching and the salvation of the Ninevites. Even then, God did not lose patience, but gently and firmly reminded Jonah of the great love that he has for all his children.

God has a purpose for each one of us and, if we listen to him and are guided by him, we will be able to join with him in his loving, saving work.

Savoury recipe: The whale

Ingredients (per whale)

- One hard-boiled egg
- Spaghetti cheese
- One black olive
- One piece of tomato or red pepper
- Lettuce

Equipment

- Knife for cutting
- Plain icing nozzle, about 4 mm wide

Preparation

If the children are very young, you might need to cut small pieces out of the olive as eyes and cut out the hollows in the egg for the blowhole and the eyes.

Crafting

1. Slice the lettuce into long strips and arrange them on a plate to look like the waves of a rough sea.
2. Cut the boiled egg in half horizontally. Cut one half into half again across the widest part.
3. Cut eyes and mouth from the olives and tomato. You can either fix them in place with mayonnaise or cut holes out of the egg using the end of a plain icing nozzle, inserting the eyes in the hollows that you have made.
4. Carefully cut a piece out of the top of the half egg with the icing nozzle. Take a 5-cm piece of spaghetti cheese and peel it until it looks like a spray of water. Place gently into the hole in the egg.
5. Put the whale body and tail on the lettuce.

Reproduced with permission from *Edible Bible Crafts* by Sally Welch, published by Barnabas for Children 2014. www.barnabasinchurches.org.uk

Sweet recipe: The whale

Ingredients (per whale)

- One fairy cake
- Vanilla buttercream icing
- Green or blue food colouring
- One Oreo cookie
- Smarties
- One small piece of strawberry lace
- Mini Smartie or chocolate drop

Equipment

- Knife for cutting and spreading

Preparation

Mix the icing with the food colouring until you have the required 'whale' colour. Split the Oreo cookie in two, and discard the half with the icing on. Carefully cut the plain half into quarters. There will inevitably be some wastage, but you can save the leftovers for crafts that need Oreo 'soil' (for example, the craft for Creation on page 22 or for Harvest on page 120).

Crafting

1. Spread the fairy cake with green or blue icing.
2. Starting in the middle of the cake, carefully place Smarties in rows to look like fish scales, covering one half of the cake. The Smarties can match the colour of the icing or simply be rainbow patterned.
3. Use the chocolate drop or mini Smartie as an eye, and bend a small piece of strawberry lace into a fishy smile.
4. Carefully wedge the Oreo cookie quarter into the end of the fairy cake to act as a tail.

Daniel

The story

When Darius the Mede became ruler, he saw that Daniel was gifted and experienced and made him one of his top three administrators.

Daniel worked hard and Darius was so impressed with him that he wanted to put Daniel in charge of the whole kingdom. But there were other officials who were jealous of Daniel...

They plotted and schemed and slowly an idea began to take shape. They went to see Darius.

'Your majesty, may you live for ever!' they said. 'We all think that you should issue a decree. No one must pray to anyone but you for the next thirty days. If they do, they should be thrown into a den of lions!'

Darius was flattered. It was a good idea, he thought. He even put it in writing so that it became law. And the law of the Medes and Persians cannot be changed.

When Daniel heard about the decree, he went as usual to his upstairs room where the windows faced Jerusalem. There he knelt down and prayed three times a day to God, asking him for help.

The men who had plotted against Daniel watched. Their plan had worked. 'Your majesty,' they said, 'are we right in thinking that anyone who disobeys your decree will be thrown into a den of lions?'

King Darius nodded. 'This decree cannot be altered,' he said.

'But Daniel, the man who has such power in your kingdom, ignores the decree. He does not pray to you. Instead he prays three times a day to his God.'

Darius was very sad. He realised that the men had set out to trap him, and now he was powerless to rescue Daniel. Darius had no choice. He ordered Daniel to be thrown into the lions' den.

'May your God save you,' he said to Daniel.

That night Darius could not sleep. As soon as it was morning, he returned to the lions' den.

'Daniel!' he cried. 'Has your God saved you from the lions?'

'Yes, your majesty!' shouted Daniel from the den. 'My God has saved me! He sent an angel to close the mouths of the hungry lions. I am unharmed.'

'Release Daniel from the den!' cried Darius, overjoyed to find Daniel alive. 'And punish those men who have tried to hurt him.'

Then Darius issued another decree.

'All the people in my kingdom must fear and respect Daniel's God. For he is the living God, whose kingdom will last for ever; he is the God who rescues and saves; he is the God who performs signs and wonders; and he has the power to save, even from the mouth of lions!'

Daniel continued faithful to God for the rest of his life.

BIBLE REFERENCE: DANIEL 6

'I make a decree, that in all my royal dominion people should tremble and fear before the God of Daniel. For he is the living God, enduring for ever. His kingdom shall never be destroyed, and his dominion has no end. He delivers and rescues, he works signs and wonders in heaven and on earth; for he has saved Daniel from the power of the lions.' (vv. 26–27)

Reflection

Daniel is one of the true heroes of the Old Testament. Although he is best-known for emerging alive from a night in a den of lions, his tale is one of courage and endurance that extended well beyond one night.

Daniel was the patient, wise adviser to no fewer

Reproduced with permission from *Edible Bible Crafts* by Sally Welch, published by Barnabas for Children 2014. www.barnabasinchurches.org.uk

than three kings—Nebuchadnezzar, Belshazzar and finally Darius. Each time, his loyalty and hard work earnt him rewards and enemies in equal measure. Each time he had to put his life in danger for the sake of his faith, and each time he convinced a king and his people of the power and might of his God.

God does not ask of us just one brave deed or one act of faith, but a continuing life of faith and goodness. We cannot manage this alone; we must call upon the Lord for his help and lean on him for support. Then the lions that threaten our lives will have their mouths shut by angels, and we will not be hurt, for we trust in God.

Savoury recipe: The lion

Ingredients (per lion)

- One rice cake
- One hard-boiled egg
- One small pepperoni sausage
- One black olive

Equipment

- Knife for cutting

Preparation

None.

Crafting

1. Remove the yolk from the egg and cut out a slice about 4 mm thick. Place the egg slice in the centre of the rice cake.
2. Slice thin pieces of pepperoni sausage and place them around the yolk as a mane.
3. Give the lion eyes and a mouth made of pieces of black olive.

Sweet recipe: The lion

Ingredients (per lion)

- One fairy cake
- Vanilla buttercream icing
- Orange or brown food colouring
- Strawberry laces
- Black writing icing

Equipment

- Knife for cutting and spreading

Preparation

Mix the icing with the food colouring until you have the required 'lion' colour.

Crafting

1. Spread the icing over the top of the fairy cake.
2. Cut the strawberry laces into pieces, roughly 15 mm long. Place these pieces round the edge of the fairy cake as a mane. You can give the lion an inner semicircle of hair for the top of his head if you like.
3. With the writing icing, give the lion eyes and a mouth.

Edible Bible crafts
New Testament

The call of the first disciples

The story

Jesus returned to Galilee and began to travel around, telling the people the good news of salvation.

'Stop doing things that are wrong; live your lives the way God wants you to. Love God and learn to love the people around you as much as you love yourself.'

Jesus watched Simon (also called Peter) and Andrew casting their nets into the waters of Lake Galilee.

'Come and follow me!' Jesus said to the two brothers. 'You can catch people for God instead of fish.'

Simon and Andrew dropped their nets and joined Jesus straight away.

Further along the lakeside, they saw James and his brother John mending their nets. Their father Zebedee was in the boat with them.

'Come and follow me!' called Jesus.

James and John got out of the boat and went with him.

These four fishermen became Jesus' first disciples. Jesus went with them to their homes in Capernaum. There Jesus taught in the synagogue. Crowds of people came to him for help and he healed those who were ill.

BIBLE REFERENCE: MATTHEW 4:17–24

As he walked by the Sea of Galilee, he saw two brothers, Simon, who is called Peter, and Andrew his brother, casting a net into the lake—for they were fishermen. And he said to them, 'Follow me, and I will make you fish for people.' Immediately they left their nets and followed him. (vv. 18–20)

Reflection

Following in footprints is an archetypal game played by small children all over the world. Wherever there is a patch of soft ground, whether it is sand, snow or earth, children delight in seeing the impression made by their feet. Even more fun is to try and walk in the footprints of the adult who is accompanying them. Stretching their legs to their fullest extent, they laugh as they try to encompass the distance between adult strides, often stumbling, occasionally losing heart, but more often getting up and trying again.

Year on year, this game becomes easier as the child's legs lengthen and their physical skills grow more refined, until they can walk with ease in the steps of those who have gone before.

We, too, stumble and trip when we first try to walk in Jesus' footsteps. The effort is great and our legs seem so short. But if we persevere, we will grow, and gradually we will find ourselves fitting more and more easily into the prints left by the Master.

Savoury recipe: Footprints

Ingredients (per foot)

- One 'cheesy foot' (see the pastry recipe on page 16)
- One slice of bread
- Pepper, celery and olives to decorate

Equipment

- Knife for cutting
- Footprint cookie cutter

Preparation

Small children may need the vegetables cut into appropriate shapes and sizes for decoration.

Crafting

1. Cut a foot shape out of the bread with the cookie cutter.
2. Place the 'cheesy foot' on the bread 'sandal'.
3. Decorate the top of the sandal any way you want.

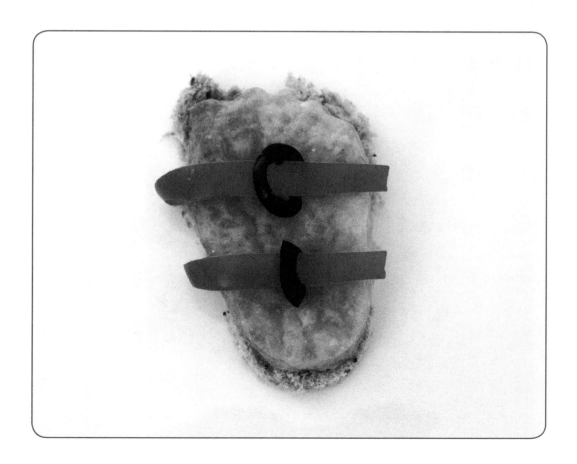

Sweet recipe: Fishing boats

Ingredients (per scene)

- One portion of blue jelly (if you cannot find any in the shops, make up some lemon jelly and add blue food colouring to the boiling water)
- Two or three grapes
- One sheet of edible paper
- Three or four Shreddies (you may need more if you find them difficult to split: see below)

Equipment

- One plastic jelly pot or bowl per person (disposable clear plastic bowls are best, as the children can see through them)
- Knife for cutting
- Scissors

Preparation

Make up the blue jelly if necessary. Small children may need help with splitting the Shreddies.

Crafting

1. Half fill the bowls with jelly that has been roughly chopped so that it looks like wave shapes.
2. Cut out sails from the edible paper.
3. Slice the grapes in half. Using the knife, make a small cut into either end of the grape. Carefully insert the sail into the cut so that it stands upright. Place the grape boats gently on the jelly sea.
4. Split the Shreddies cereal so that there is only one layer of gridwork. Place each grid against the side of one of the boats so that it looks like a fishing net that has just been thrown overboard.

The two houses

The story

As people listened to what Jesus had to say, the people divided into groups. Many were eager to hear more. They wanted to know how to please God. Some were suspicious or angry at this way of teaching. It was different from the teaching of the scribes and Pharisees. So Jesus told a story.

'If you listen to me and do what I say, you will be like a wise man who built his house on a rock. Before he started work, the man made sure that his house had firm foundations on the rock. Then when the rain battered against the house, and the wind blew around it, it did not collapse. It remained firm and solid.

'If you take no notice of what I have said, you will be like a foolish man who built his house on sand. When the wind blew and the rain beat against his house, it had no foundations and so it fell down. The walls and roof, the door and all his belongings were swept away.

'Don't be like the foolish man, regretting his mistake when it is too late to change things. Be like the wise man; listen well and act on what you hear.'

BIBLE REFERENCE: MATTHEW 7:24–27

'Everyone then who hears these words of mine and acts on them will be like a wise man who built his house on rock. The rain fell, the floods came, and the winds blew and beat on that house, but it did not fall, because it had been founded on rock.' (vv. 24–25)

Reflection

This parable seems to be telling us a way of getting into heaven by the sweat of our brow. It seems to be saying that if we work hard (pray, come to church, give to charity), we will be saved. The storm won't get us.

However, we forget that the foundation of rock is not something that the man has to work at. It is given to him. All he has to do is choose the site. The parable doesn't say anything about the man labouring hard to build the house on rock foundations: we add that on afterwards.

The rock foundations are the great gift of God's love. All our spirituality will be built on the rock of being children of God—of being already saved, through no effort of our own, but totally through the free gift of God's great love for us. We can choose what sort of house to build, and we hope to build a good strong one, but, whatever happens, the foundations are there. When the storms of life hit (and they will hit, however much we hope they won't), maybe through bad choices, maybe through absolutely no fault of ours, the house will not crumble because it is built on the firm foundations and eternal rock of Christ, his love for us and his sacrifice for us.

Reproduced with permission from *Edible Bible Crafts* by Sally Welch, published by Barnabas for Children 2014. www.barnabasinchurches.org.uk

Savoury recipe: The two houses

Ingredients (for both houses)

- One quantity of rice boiled in water to which blue food colouring has been added
- Nine or ten small, square savoury biscuits per house
- One dsp Parmesan cheese (a cheaper alternative is cheese biscuits, finely crumbled)
- One rice cake, ideally rectangular rather than round
- Squirty mayonnaise or cheese (mayonnaise is easier to work with)
- Slices of carrot and peppers (optional)

Equipment

- None

Preparation

None.

Crafting

1. Build a small house on top of the rice cake, using the squirty mayonnaise to glue the square cheese biscuits together.
2. Place the rice cake on a plate. Next to the rice cake put a small heap of Parmesan cheese or finely crushed cheese biscuits.
3. Lay a couple of square biscuits on top to look like a collapsed version of the other house.
4. Carefully spread the blue rice all around the two houses.
5. Older children may wish to fill the garden with flowers and plants cut out of carrot and red and green pepper slices.

Reproduced with permission from *Edible Bible Crafts* by Sally Welch, published by Barnabas for Children 2014. www.barnabasinchurches.org.uk

Sweet recipe: The house on the rock

Ingredients (per house)

- Two or three thin slices of sponge cake cooked in a loaf tin
- One Scotch pancake (the larger size is better)
- One digestive or other round biscuit
- One quantity of vanilla buttercream icing
- Blue and black food colouring

Equipment

- Knife for spreading

Preparation

Divide the vanilla buttercream icing into three, with one part being smaller than the rest. Mix one of the larger quantities with black colouring until you have a grey, rock-like colour. Mix the other large quantity with blue to make a sea colour.

Crafting

1. Place the Scotch pancake on a plate and spread the blue icing over it, making the icing look like waves.
2. Spread grey icing over the digestive biscuit as the rock base for the house. Place the iced biscuit on top of the pancake.
3. Cut the sponge into four small rectangles.
4. Build the house on the biscuit rock, using the plain vanilla buttercream icing as cement.

Reproduced with permission from *Edible Bible Crafts* by Sally Welch, published by Barnabas for Children 2014. www.barnabasinchurches.org.uk

The sower and the seed

● ●

The story

Jesus taught the people using parables, stories about things they understood but with a special meaning.

'A farmer went out to sow some seed,' began Jesus. 'He took handfuls of seed and cast it from side to side as he walked along.

'Some seed fell on the path. Birds came and quickly gobbled it up.

'Some seed fell on soil that was full of stones. The seed began to grow quite quickly, but it did not last long. Its roots had not stretched down deep into the soil so that when the sun beat down upon it, the plants shrivelled up and died.

'Some seed landed among thorns and as it grew up, it was choked by the thorns so it could not produce fruit.

'But some seed fell on good rich soil. There it began to grow, strong and healthy, until eventually it produced a good harvest.'…

Later, when the disciples were alone with Jesus, they asked him what the story about the farmer and the seed meant.

'The farmer who sows the seed is like God planting his message of truth in those who hear it,' Jesus said.

'Some people who hear the message are like the soil on the path. They hear the message about God, but quickly forget about him.

'Some people are like the stony soil. They try to obey God, but give up when things get difficult or people criticise them for their faith.

'Some are like the seed that fell among thorns. They try to follow God, but become distracted by money or other worries and their faith is choked.

'But others are like the good rich soil. They hear the word and grow up like strong healthy plants, living fruitful lives that God can use, not being swayed by the cares of the world, and sharing their faith with others.'

BIBLE REFERENCE: MARK 4:3–20

'And these are the ones sown on the good soil: they hear the word and accept it and bear fruit, thirty and sixty and a hundredfold.' (v. 20)

Reflection

A firm favourite at harvest time, this parable has the advantage of having been explained for us by Jesus himself. Although it will be familiar to most people, one aspect that is sometimes forgotten is our responsibility to care for those people around us who hear the word of God. Whether we share the same 'soil' as them or not, we can help the word to take root and grow by supporting and encouraging others in their faith journey, while ensuring that we are not so engaged in helping the spiritual life of others to grow and develop that we neglect our own.

Reproduced with permission from *Edible Bible Crafts* by Sally Welch, published by Barnabas for Children 2014. www.barnabasinchurches.org.uk

Savoury recipe: A bird

Ingredients (per bird)

- One slice of bread or one round rice cake
- One slice of salami
- One piece of yellow pepper or cheese or carrot
- One hard-boiled egg
- Two black olives

Equipment

- Knife for cutting
- Circular cake cutter (optional)

Preparation

Young children might need the shapes cut out for them beforehand.

Crafting

1. Cut a circle out of the bread, the same size as the salami slice.
2. Cut a triangular-shaped wedge out of the salami and place the larger piece on the bread. The smaller piece of salami can be cut into tail feathers and put at the edge of the bread.
3. Cut a triangular 'beak' from the carrot/cheese/pepper.
4. Cut oval eyes from slices of the white of the hard-boiled egg. Pupils can be cut from the olives.

Reproduced with permission from *Edible Bible Crafts* by Sally Welch, published by Barnabas for Children 2014. www.barnabasinchurches.org.uk

Sweet recipe: Basket of seed

Note: This craft requires some dexterity and is not suitable for very young children.

Ingredients (per basket)

- One slice of apple, about 2.5 cm thick
- Thin stick biscuits (Mikado biscuits or similar)
- Two Fruit Winders
- Sunflower seeds

Equipment

- Circular cutter (optional)

Preparation

None.

Crafting

1. Cut the top third off the biscuits. This must be done carefully or the biscuits will break.
2. Insert the biscuits into the apple slice, like a fence around the edge, as close together as possible.
3. Weave the Fruit Winders in and out of the biscuits.
4. Fill the completed basket with seeds.

Reproduced with permission from *Edible Bible Crafts* by Sally Welch, published by Barnabas for Children 2014. www.barnabasinchurches.org.uk

The treasure in the field

The story

Jesus told other stories to explain what God's kingdom was like.

'Imagine that there is some treasure hidden in a field. One day, a man accidentally finds the treasure. He buries it again quickly, then goes back home. He sells his home, his furniture, his cooking pots—even his donkey—so that he can buy the field. Then the treasure is his, and nothing could be worth more than that.'

The people listened. Some of them understood. Jesus meant that God's kingdom was more valuable than anything they owned. It was worth doing anything to be part of it.

BIBLE REFERENCE: MATTHEW 13:44

> 'The kingdom of heaven is like treasure hidden in a field, which someone found and hid; then in his joy he goes and sells all that he has and buys that field.'

Reflection

The treasure hidden in a field is just one metaphor, or comparison, that Matthew uses when writing about the kingdom of God—including hidden coins, a precious pearl, a net, mustard seed, yeast, light, a harvest, a royal feast, a party. Using metaphors is the best a finite mind can do with an infinite subject.

These comparisons are difficult to understand, and perhaps the best approach is not to seek to understand them completely but to hold them in tension in the mind. The kingdom of God is beyond history, not part of it; it is dynamic, not static; it is a divine gift, not a human achievement. It is given to us through grace, and what we must do, with the help of that same grace, is to respond.

In this parable, Jesus is trying to tell us that there is something beyond us, of the Spirit, that is worth everything we have. When the opportunity to grasp it comes to us, we must not let it go by, but we should pick it up and hold on to it for ever.

Reproduced with permission from *Edible Bible Crafts* by Sally Welch, published by Barnabas for Children 2014. www.barnabasinchurches.org.uk

Savoury recipe: Hidden treasure

Ingredients (per treasure)

- Two slices of bread
- Two or three lettuce leaves
- A slice of red pepper

Equipment

- Knife for carving (ideally, some of the tools that are available for carving pumpkins)

Preparation

None.

Crafting

1. Slice the lettuce and scatter it on a plate to look like a grassy meadow.
2. Cut the crusts from the two slices of bread. Place the bread slices one on top of the other.
3. With the edge of a chopping board or similar, squash the edges of three sides of the bread slices together to form a packet with an opening at one end.
4. Carve a heart from the slice of red pepper. Carefully place the heart inside the bread packet, making sure not to split open the side 'seams'.
5. Seal the final edge of the packet and place gently in the lettuce field.

Sweet recipe: Hidden treasure

Ingredients (per treasure)

- One fairy cake
- Green fondant icing, or white icing that has been coloured grass green
- One jewelled cake decoration (sugar diamonds or any small attractive sweet)

Equipment

- Circular cutters, ideally one the size of the fairy cake and one much smaller
- Rolling pin
- Baking paper

Preparation

Small children may need the fondant icing rolled out into fairy cake-sized circles.

Crafting

1. With the smaller cutter, cut a small hole from the centre of the fairy cake and put the cut-out piece to one side.
2. Roll out a piece of fondant icing and cut to the same size as the fairy cake.
3. Cut a central hole out from the icing with the smaller cutter and place on top of the cake circle that has been set aside. Put the larger piece of icing on the fairy cake.
4. Place the treasure at the bottom of the hole in the fairy cake. Put the cut-out piece of cake on top, burying the treasure.

Calming the storm

The story

It was evening, and Jesus was tired after teaching the crowds of people all day.

'Let's cross to the other side of the lake,' Jesus said to his friends. So they prepared the boat and set sail.

Jesus went to the stern of the boat and lay down, a cushion under his head. He was soon fast asleep.

At first the boat bobbed up and down gently and rhythmically. Jesus' friends thought about all they had seen and heard during the day as they made progress across Lake Galilee. But then, as so often happened on that stretch of water, the wind suddenly changed direction. The waves began to crash over the side and the boat lurched dangerously up and down.

The men clung to the mast of the boat. Even the fishermen among them knew they were in danger. They felt sure they were going to drown. But Jesus was still fast asleep.

'Master, help us!' they shouted, waking him. 'Don't you care if we die?'

Jesus stood up. He spoke to the winds and the waves. 'Be calm!' he said. The wind dropped and the sea was still.

Then Jesus turned to look at his frightened disciples. 'Why are you afraid?' he asked. 'Don't you trust me?'

Jesus' friends were amazed. They had no idea he had so much power. 'Who is he?' they asked one another. 'Even the wind and waves do what he says.'

BIBLE REFERENCE: MARK 4:35–41

He woke up and rebuked the wind, and said to the sea, 'Peace, be still!' Then the wind ceased, and there was a dead calm. He said to them, 'Why are you afraid? Have you still no faith?' (vv. 39–40)

Reflection

It would be so easy for us if only we had more faith! The obstacles and stresses of daily life, the pain and hardship of some of the difficulties that come our way, would be faced with a calm confidence that God was with us, walking alongside us in our darkest times, his love a constant reassurance to us.

There may be some people whose faith is that great, that strong. But many of us find ourselves in times of trouble in a very different situation, frightened by the events that have befallen us, terrified by the thought that we are facing them on our own. At times like these, this story can be a tremendous reminder of the loving presence of God at all times, and we can repeat to ourselves the well-loved phrase of Jesus that is both a rebuke and a promise: 'Why are you afraid? Have you still no faith?'

Reproduced with permission from *Edible Bible Crafts* by Sally Welch, published by Barnabas for Children 2014. www.barnabasinchurches.org.uk

Savoury recipe: Fishing boat

Ingredients (per boat)

- One small soft bread roll
- One olive
- One Twiglet or stick of celery
- One slice of ham
- One stick of celery

Equipment

- Knife for cutting

Preparation

None.

Crafting

1. Cut the bread roll in half horizontally.
2. Pull out a small piece of bread from the centre of the roll and fit the olive into the gap. The olive needs to fit quite snugly.
3. Cut out a piece of ham to be the sail and fit to the Twiglet or celery stick mast.
4. Slice the celery stick and place the pieces around the roll so that they look like rough waves.

Reproduced with permission from *Edible Bible Crafts* by Sally Welch, published by Barnabas for Children 2014. www.barnabasinchurches.org.uk

Sweet recipe: Fishing boat

Note: This craft is interchangeable with the one for 'The call of the first disciples' (page 60), so the alternative can be used if there are allergies to kiwi fruit among your crafters.

Ingredients (per boat)

- One portion of blue jelly (if you cannot find any in the shops, make up some lemon jelly and add blue food colouring to the boiling water)
- One kiwi fruit
- One sheet of edible paper
- One thin stick biscuit (Mikado biscuits work well)

Equipment

- One plastic jelly pot or bowl per person (disposable clear plastic bowls are best, as the children can see through them)
- Knife for cutting
- Scissors

Preparation

None, unless you need to make up the blue jelly.

Crafting

1. Half fill the bowls with jelly, roughly chopped so that it looks like wave shapes.
2. Cut out sails from the edible paper.
3. Slice the kiwi fruit in half and hollow out the centre of one half so that it looks like the inside of a boat.
4. Cut out a sail from the paper and mount it on the biscuit stick. Push the biscuit stick mast into the base of the kiwi fruit boat.
5. Place the boat gently on the jelly sea.

Reproduced with permission from *Edible Bible Crafts* by Sally Welch, published by Barnabas for Children 2014. www.barnabasinchurches.org.uk

Feeding the five thousand

The story

Jesus went by boat into the hills on the far side of Lake Galilee. When he found people waiting for him even there, he could not turn them away. He healed those who were ill until late in the day.

Then Jesus looked at how many had come. There were more than 5000 men, plus the women and children. Jesus turned to Philip, who came from nearby Bethsaida.

'Do you know where we could buy bread for all these people?' Jesus asked.

'It would cost far too much to buy bread for this number!' answered Philip.

Then Andrew, another of Jesus' friends, noticed a boy in the crowd who had with him a picnic lunch of five small barley rolls and two little fish. He brought the boy to Jesus.

'This boy has some food,' he said 'but it won't go very far!'

Jesus took the food he was offered. 'Ask the people to sit down,' he said to his friends.

The people sat down on the grass and watched as Jesus took the food and asked God to bless it. Then he began to break the bread and fish into pieces, and passed it to his friends, who shared it again with the people.

The people shared the food among themselves and ate until they were no longer hungry. Then Jesus' friends went among the people picking up anything that was left over. They collected twelve baskets full of leftover pieces.

Over 5000 people ate that day and had more than enough to eat.

BIBLE REFERENCE: JOHN 6:1–14

When they were satisfied, he told his disciples, 'Gather up the fragments left over, so that nothing may be lost.' So they gathered them up, and from the fragments of the five barley loaves, left by those who had eaten, they filled twelve baskets. When the people saw the sign that he had done, they began to say, 'This is indeed the prophet who is to come into the world.' (vv. 12–14)

Reflection

The feeding of the large crowd, as John calls it, is the only miracle of Jesus that is described in all four Gospels and for this reason alone it is significant—but there is more. There is something timeless about this tale that not only captured the four Gospel writers but can still speak to us today. First, the story shows us that Jesus is able to satisfy every type of hunger we have, both physical and spiritual. It shows us not only God's power at work in Jesus but God's care as well. God reaches out through Jesus to meet the needs of those who are following him. Even more wonderfully than that, Jesus is able to take what is offered to him and multiply it, so that what at first seemed to be not enough ends up being more than enough.

So often in our daily lives we are overwhelmed by the problems that surround us, both global and domestic. We would like to do more, be more, help more, but we are afraid that we will prove inadequate and our resources insufficient. The feeding of the five thousand teaches us that all we have to do is bring what we have, just like the boy on the hillside with his loaves and fish. We bring it not thinking about what it might or might not be able to do, but focusing instead on who we bring it to—God and his great love.

Savoury recipe: The big picnic

Ingredients (per picnic)

- One tortilla
- One piece of cucumber with its skin on
- A carrot
- Small cheesy biscuits
- One ready-made croustade (available from supermarkets, for canapés)

Equipment

- Knife for carving (ideally, some of the tools that are available for carving pumpkins)

Preparation

Small children may need the strips peeled from the cucumber for them.

Crafting

1. Cut the tortilla into a square.
2. Carefully peel strips of skin from the cucumber, as long as possible. Put the cucumber strips on to the tortilla to look like a woven pattern.
3. Carve fish from two slices of carrot.
4. Put the fish and the cheesy biscuits into the croustade (or carve a basket from a chunk of cucumber).

Sweet recipe: The big picnic

Ingredients (per picnic)

- One digestive biscuit or home-made biscuit (see recipe on page 16)
- One Fruit Winder
- One croustade (available from supermarkets, for canapés)
- Fondant icing in ivory and orange (or other bread and fish colours, such as brown and yellow)

Equipment

- Knife for carving

Preparation

None.

Crafting

1. Cut the Fruit Winder into strips slightly longer than the biscuit.
2. Lay the strips on to the biscuit to form a woven pattern. Older children can actually weave the strips together.
3. Fashion fish and bread from the fondant icing and place them in the croustade basket (or make a basket from the spare fondant).

Reproduced with permission from *Edible Bible Crafts* by Sally Welch, published by Barnabas for Children 2014. www.barnabasinchurches.org.uk

The good Samaritan

The story

One day a man came to Jesus to see how he would answer questions about God's laws…

'Teacher,' he said. 'What must I do to live with God for ever?'

'What does God's law say?' Jesus asked the man.

'Love God with all your heart, your soul, your strength and your mind. Love your neighbour as you love yourself,' replied the man.

'Then you know the answer,' said Jesus. 'Do it and you will live with God for ever.'

'But who is my neighbour?' asked the man.

'I will tell you a story,' said Jesus. 'There was once a man who was walking on the lonely road from Jerusalem to Jericho. He was attacked by some robbers, who stole his money and took his clothes and left him half dead by the side of the road.

'Later on, a priest came along the same road. He saw the injured man, but decided not to help him. He walked past on the other side.

'Some time later, a Levite came along the road. He also saw the wounded man, but did not stop to help.

'Finally, a Samaritan came along the road. As soon as he saw the man lying there, he stopped. He bandaged his wounds, he helped him on to his own donkey, and took him to an inn. He gave the innkeeper some money, and asked him to look after the injured man till he was well again. "When I return I will give you any more money you need," he said.'

Then Jesus asked the man who was listening to the story: 'Who was a good neighbour to the wounded man?'

'The one who helped him,' said the man.

'You must do the same as him,' said Jesus.

BIBLE REFERENCE: LUKE 10:25–37

'Which of these three, do you think, was a neighbour to the man who fell into the hands of the robbers?' He said, 'The one who showed him mercy.' Jesus said to him, 'Go and do likewise.' (vv. 36–37)

Reflection

The question that the lawyer asks of Jesus—'Who is my neighbour?'—and Jesus' reply in the form of this parable are vitally important to the Christian faith, and it is fortunate that this parable is so compelling and lively, since it should be told at every opportunity.

The danger of becoming absorbed by one particular group of people to the exclusion of all others is very great, especially since, in today's fragmented society, we may be tempted to cling more strongly to the groups we do belong to. The good Samaritan is a reminder that we should be concerned with the welfare of all people and wary of judging those who do not share our interests.

Savoury recipe: The man attacked by robbers

Ingredients (per man)

- Two tortillas
- 12 small square cheese biscuits
- Squirty cheese
- One slice of radish or one small round cheese
- Scraps of black olive, carrot or pepper for the features

Equipment

- Knife for cutting and spreading

Preparation

Young children might need the features cut out for them beforehand.

Crafting

1. Cut one of the tortillas into a square. Spread the square with squirty cheese.
2. Arrange the cheese biscuits on top of the cheese to look like a patchwork quilt.
3. Using the slice of radish or round cheese as a head, give the man some features using the scraps of olive and peppers. You could use a piece of parsley for hair if you like.

Reproduced with permission from *Edible Bible Crafts* by Sally Welch, published by Barnabas for Children 2014. www.barnabasinchurches.org.uk

Sweet recipe:
The robbers

Ingredients (per scene)

- Two digestive biscuits
- Vanilla buttercream icing
- Black food colouring
- Fondant icing of different colours, including pink

Equipment

- Knife for spreading
- Rolling pin

Preparation

None.

Crafting

1. Crush one of the digestive biscuits with the rolling pin, to make fine crumbs.
2. Mix a small amount of vanilla buttercream icing with the colouring until it is grey. Spread a thin line of this icing down the middle of the biscuit to form the road.
3. Spread either side of the road with plain vanilla buttercream icing.
4. Scatter the biscuit crumbs carefully on to the icing, trying to avoid the 'road'.
5. With the coloured fondant icing, mould the scene of the attack.

The lost sheep

The story

Many of the Pharisees and teachers of the law criticised Jesus because he spent time with ordinary people, many of whom they thought were sinners, doing things that were wrong.

'If you owned 100 sheep,' Jesus said to them, 'and one of them was lost, what would you do? Leave it to die and be content with the 99 that are safe in the sheep pen? No, you would go in search of the one that was lost. You would look everywhere until it was found, then you would be happier over that one lost sheep than all the others. So it is with God. He cares about all the sheep, and will not be happy till he has saved the one who has wandered away from the right path.'

BIBLE REFERENCE: MATTHEW 18:12–14

'What do you think? If a shepherd has a hundred sheep, and one of them has gone astray, does he not leave the ninety-nine on the mountains and go in search of the one that went astray?' (v. 12)

Reflection

One of the most compelling aspects of the Christian faith is the message that every single person matters to God. In a world where the needs and happiness of the individual are often sacrificed to the larger institution or organisation, Jesus emphasises that it does not matter how small or insignificant we may feel: in God's eyes we are all equal, all special and all loved.

The story of the tremendous efforts the shepherd makes to find the one sheep that has got lost emphasises God's concern for every single one of us. Young children can often feel that they don't matter in a world that is organised and run by adults. The story of the lost sheep reminds them of their importance to God—and reminds the grown-ups, too.

Reproduced with permission from *Edible Bible Crafts* by Sally Welch, published by Barnabas for Children 2014. www.barnabasinchurches.org.uk

Savoury recipe: The lost sheep

Ingredients (per sheep)

- One large plain rice cake (if you can buy the rectangular ones, they will look more like a field)
- One dsp mayonnaise
- Green food colouring
- One slice white bread
- One black olive
- Two or three raisins
- One slice processed cheese (optional)

Equipment

- Large and small flower-shaped cutters
- Knife

Preparation

Mix the mayonnaise with the food colouring until it looks grass-green. If the children are very young, slice some olives to make the curly hair.

Crafting

1. Spread the green mayonnaise over the rice cake.
2. Cut one large and one small flower shape from the slice of bread.
3. Position the bread flowers on to the rice cake so that they look like a sheep's head and body. You may want to cut a piece out of the sheep's head so that it fits snugly on to the body.
3. If you wish, cut out a flower shape from a slice of processed cheese and place it on top of the bread body.
4. Add raisins or olives for legs, and olive slices for curly black hair (if not using cheese). Use chopped raisins or olives for eyes and a mouth. For a really good eye, use the end of an icing nozzle to cut out a circle from an olive.

Reproduced with permission from *Edible Bible Crafts* by Sally Welch, published by Barnabas for Children 2014. www.barnabasinchurches.org.uk

Sweet recipe:
The lost sheep

Ingredients (per sheep)

- Two fairy cakes
- One dsp vanilla buttercream icing
- Green food colouring
- Six mini marshmallows
- Black writing icing
- Black fondant icing (optional)

Equipment

- Knife for spreading
- Scissors

Preparation

Mix the green food colouring with the vanilla butter-cream icing to make a grass-green colour.

Crafting

1. Cover the tops of both fairy cakes with green vanilla icing. Place five marshmallows on one 'field', and one marshmallow on the other.
2. With the writing icing, carefully place a small blob at one end of each marshmallow. This will be the sheep's head.
3. Older children may like to make small balls out of the black fondant icing and stick them on to the marshmallows with black writing icing.

The good shepherd

The story

'I am like a good shepherd,' Jesus said. 'I know all my sheep by name and care about them; they know my voice and know they can come to me and I will lead them to good pasture. I will give my sheep everything they need and much more besides.

'Like a good shepherd, I love my sheep and will let no harm come to them. When someone who is not a real shepherd looks after the sheep, he runs away if a wolf comes and attacks the flock. He doesn't really care about them. But I am willing to die for my sheep.

'I am the good shepherd. I know my sheep and my sheep know me. I have other sheep too who are not in the same sheepfold. One day there will be one great flock, all led by one shepherd. I will lay down my life for the sheep; no one will take my life from me. Then I will take up my life again.'

BIBLE REFERENCE: JOHN 10:11–18

'I am the good shepherd. The good shepherd lays down his life for the sheep.' (v. 11)

Reflection

The metaphor of the good shepherd is a powerful one. The image of a man who knows every single one of his sheep by name and cares about them all as individuals is very evocative.

God watches over and protects his flock. When we cry out, he comes to us; when we look for him, he will be there; but the best thing is that when we stray from him, he will come and look for us.

It is easy to get lost in this world, to spend our lives rushing back and forth with all the things we have to do, so busy that we lose sight of what is important and small things become great things. Then we lose our sense of who we are and why we are here. At these times, what we must do is stop and allow ourselves to be refreshed by the presence of God, to enjoy the green pastures and still waters of his love and his peace before we continue our daily lives.

Savoury recipe: The shepherd

Ingredients (per shepherd)

- Spaghetti cheese
- One Twiglet
- Some lettuce
- One slice of bread
- Scraps of black olive and tomato

Equipment

- Knife for cutting
- Small flower-shaped cookie cutters, in two sizes

Preparation

None.

Crafting

1. Slice the lettuce and place it at the bottom of a plate as grass.
2. With the cutters, cut one larger and one smaller shape per sheep out of the bread and fit them together on the lettuce. Use scraps of olive for the eyes.
3. To make the shepherd, first take the spaghetti cheese and fray the end to look like hair.
4. Carefully peel two 'arms' away from the middle of the spaghetti cheese. Carefully split the bottom of the spaghetti cheese in two to make legs.
5. Arrange the shepherd on the lettuce 'grass'. You can give him olive and tomato features. Place a Twiglet by his side as his shepherd's crook.

Reproduced with permission from *Edible Bible Crafts* by Sally Welch, published by Barnabas for Children 2014. www.barnabasinchurches.org.uk

Sweet recipe: The sheep

Ingredients (per sheep)

- One fairy cake
- Vanilla buttercream icing
- Black writing icing
- Two chocolate drops (optional)
- Mini marshmallows

Equipment

- Knife for spreading

Preparation

None.

Crafting

1. Spread vanilla buttercream icing over the top of the fairy cake.
2. Cut the marshmallows in half. Carefully arrange them round the edge of the fairy cake to make the sheep's wool.
3. Add features using writing icing. You can use chocolate drops for eyes if preferred.

The prodigal son

The story

There was once a man with two sons. One day, the younger son said to his father, 'Let me have my share of everything I will inherit when you die. I'd like to travel and enjoy myself now.' So the father divided everything that he had between his two sons.

The younger son took his money and went far away. He used all his money enjoying himself and making lots of friends, but after a time he had spent it all.

Then there was a terrible famine in the land. There was nothing to eat. The younger son took the only job he could find, feeding pigs. He was so hungry, he could have eaten the pigs' food. Then the young man realised how silly he was.

'The people who work for my father have far more than I have now. I'll go home and tell him I am sorry. I will ask if I can have a job on the farm.'

But the boy's father had been watching and waiting, hoping his son would come back. He saw his son coming and ran to meet him. He threw his arms around him and hugged him.

'I have let you down and done things I am ashamed of,' the boy said. 'I am so sorry. I don't deserve to be treated as your son. Let me work for you instead.'

But his father shook his head.

'Fetch the best clothes for my son,' the father called to one of his servants. 'Find new sandals and a ring for his finger. Prepare the best food! I thought my son was dead. He was lost, but now he's found. Let's have a party to celebrate his return!'

BIBLE REFERENCE: LUKE 15:11–32

'But we had to celebrate and rejoice, because this brother of yours was dead and has come to life; he was lost and has been found.' (v. 32)

Reflection

The three characters in this parable are each powerful illustrations of gospel—or not so gospel—behaviour. We can reflect on the loving patience of the father, who gives his son the freedom to choose his own path but watches constantly for his return, and is gracious and liberal with his welcome when at last the penitent is in sight. We can put ourselves in the place of the prodigal who, at last, after much wasted time, turns again to his true home and finds peace and acceptance there. We can empathise perhaps with the elder son, who has lost sight of the grace that is so abundant in all God's dealings with his children and has to be gently reminded that all are sinners. If we take this story to heart, there is much to learn from it.

Reproduced with permission from *Edible Bible Crafts* by Sally Welch, published by Barnabas for Children 2014. www.barnabasinchurches.org.uk

Savoury recipe:
The pig

Ingredients (per pig)

- One rice cake
- One slice of bread
- One small pepperoni sausage
- One black olive

Equipment

- Knife for cutting
- Three round cookie cutters in different sizes

Preparation

None.

Crafting

1. Cut out three different-sized circles from the bread and place them on top of the rice cake in descending size order.
2. Cut a slice of pepperoni sausage in half and place each half at the edge of the middle-sized circle of bread, as ears.
3. Put two slices of sausage on the smallest bread circle, as nostrils. Use the olive to make a smiley mouth, eyes and a tail.

Sweet recipe: The pig

Ingredients (per pig)

- One fairy cake
- Pink fondant icing
- Black writing icing
- Four chocolate drops (optional)
- One marshmallow

Equipment

- Rolling pin
- Circular cookie cutter, the same size as the top of the fairy cake

Preparation

None.

Crafting

1. Roll out the fondant icing and cut out a circle. Place it on the fairy cake.
2. Slice the marshmallow in half horizontally and put one half in the centre of the fairy cake as a snout.
3. Slice the other half in two down the middle and put at the edge of the fairy cake as ears.
4. With the writing icing or chocolate drops, make nostrils and eyes.

87

Ten men with leprosy

The story

As Jesus passed near the border of Samaria and Galilee, he saw ten men standing together in a huddle. They were dressed in rags and had covered their faces and their damaged limbs. Jesus knew that they had the skin disease called leprosy that made them outcasts.

They called to Jesus from a distance. 'Jesus! Please heal us!'

Jesus knew how much they suffered and wanted to help them.

'Go to the priest,' Jesus told them. 'Show him your skin.'

The ten men turned to walk away but as they did so, they realised that they had been healed. Their skin was healthy. The leprosy had gone!

One of the men was from Samaria. He turned back to Jesus, praising God, and knelt at Jesus' feet. 'Thank you, Master! Thank you!' he said.

Jesus looked at the man on his knees and he looked into the distance at those who were still walking away.

'Were there not ten men who needed help?' said Jesus. 'Are you the only one who came back to thank God? Go home now. You are well because you believed that God could heal you.'

BIBLE REFERENCE: LUKE 17:11–19

> Then Jesus asked, 'Were not ten made clean? But the other nine, where are they? Was none of them found to return and give praise to God except this foreigner?' Then he said to him, 'Get up and go on your way; your faith has made you well.' (vv. 17–19)

Reflection

One of the most important tasks we do in educating small children is teaching them to say 'thank you'. Why is it so important? Because it teaches them that the person who has just helped them or given them a drink is another person just like them. It helps them to recognise others as being significant as well as themselves.

The man with leprosy who turned back to thank Jesus appreciated what the other nine did not—the difference between 'This thing has been done for me' and '*You* did this thing for me'. It is our duty as Christians to recognise our common humanity with all people. Jesus thought the leprous Samaritan worth healing. The formerly leprous Samaritan thought Jesus worth thanking, and for that he was saved. The Christian faith makes possible, makes obligatory, a new way of looking at people. 'Thank you' is just the beginning.

Savoury recipe: Man with leprosy

Ingredients (per man)

- One cheesy man (see the pastry recipe on page 16)
- One black olive
- One small pepperoni sausage
- Tomato ketchup (optional)

Equipment

- Knife for cutting
- Piping bag (optional)
- Cookie cutter

Preparation

Snip the end off the piping bag and fill it with a tablespoon of tomato ketchup (if using).

Crafting

1. Slice the pepperoni and place the slices on the man's body as buttons.
2. With the olive, make eyes and an unhappy mouth.
3. For the more bloodthirsty crafters, you can cut off a piece of arm or leg and edge the wound with tomato ketchup.

Reproduced with permission from *Edible Bible Crafts* by Sally Welch, published by Barnabas for Children 2014. www.barnabasinchurches.org.uk

Sweet recipe: Man with leprosy

Ingredients (per man)

- One man-shaped biscuit (see recipe on page 16)
- Writing icing in different colours

Equipment

- None

Preparation

None.

Crafting

1. Decorate the man with writing icing, giving him unhappy features and raggedy clothes.
2. You can give him wounds edged with blood if the occasion demands it.

Blind Bartimaeus

The story

Bartimaeus was begging at the side of the road when Jesus and his friends went to Jericho. Bartimaeus was blind, but he heard the crowd who were following Jesus. He knew something unusual was happening.

'Who's passing by?' he shouted out. 'What's happening?'

'It's Jesus,' someone answered him. 'The teacher from Nazareth is here in Jericho!'

Bartimaeus had heard all about Jesus. He knew that he had made a paralysed man walk and helped a deaf man hear.

'Help me!' he shouted out. 'Jesus, have pity on me!'

'Be quiet!' said someone else in the crowd.

'Stop shouting!' said another.

But Bartimaeus would not stop. He shouted even louder. 'Jesus! Help me!'

Jesus heard Bartimaeus and stopped. 'Tell him to come to me,' he said.

'It's OK!' someone told Bartimaeus. 'Jesus has heard you. He's asking for you!'

Bartimaeus threw off his cloak and jumped to his feet. He felt his way through the crowd, until he came to Jesus.

'How can I help you?' asked Jesus.

'I want to see again,' said Bartimaeus.

'Then you shall see,' replied Jesus. 'Go now. You believed I could make you well. You can have what you asked for.'

Bartimaeus was blind no longer! He could see! He didn't return to his place on the roadside to beg; now Bartimaeus joined the crowd of people following Jesus.

BIBLE REFERENCE: MARK 10:46–52

Jesus said to him, 'Go; your faith has made you well.' Immediately he regained his sight and followed him on the way. (v. 52)

Reflection

On the way to Jerusalem, Jesus heals a blind beggar—not so uncommon, as Jesus had been healing many people. But it is Bartimaeus' faith that has enabled him to see, because, although he is physically blind, he can still recognise Jesus as the Son of God.

Throughout their time with Jesus, even the disciples were slow to recognise Jesus in this way. Ultimately they identified him through all the things he did in their presence—teaching and healing, loving and forgiving.

Christ is here today, wherever we are right now and wherever we go. Christ will appear before us as we talk and work with the people around us. Let us make each moment a miracle of sight as we see Christ in the faces of those around us and celebrate the extraordinary within the everyday.

Reproduced with permission from *Edible Bible Crafts* by Sally Welch, published by Barnabas for Children 2014. www.barnabasinchurches.org.uk

Savoury recipe: Bartimaeus' eye

Ingredients (per eye)

- One small round bread roll
- One piece of red pepper
- One piece of green pepper
- One black olive
- Either one piece of salami or some tomato pizza topping and grated cheese

Equipment

- Knife for cutting
- Cookie cutter

Preparation

If you are using the pizza option, split the bread roll horizontally and spread on the pizza topping. Sprinkle with grated cheese and toast.

Small children may need help to cut out 'eye' shapes from the peppers.

Crafting

1. If using the salami option, split the bread roll horizontally and place a slice of salami on one half, then follow the instructions below. If using the pizza option, follow the instructions below.
2. Carefully cut an eye shape from the red pepper, then a smaller eye shape from the green pepper. Cut a small hole from the centre of the green pepper eye, and a hole the same size as the green pepper eye from the red pepper.
3. Place the red pepper on the bread roll.
4. Insert the green pepper into the space in the red pepper.
5. Place the olive in the hole in the green pepper.

Reproduced with permission from *Edible Bible Crafts* by Sally Welch, published by Barnabas for Children 2014. www.barnabasinchurches.org.uk

Sweet recipe: Bartimaeus' eye

Ingredients (per eye)

- One biscuit (see recipe on page 16)
- Writing icing
- One slice kiwi fruit
- One blueberry

Equipment

- Knife for cutting

Preparation

None.

Crafting

1. Slice a thin piece of kiwi fruit and hollow out a small piece from the centre. Place the kiwi fruit on the biscuit.
2. Cut a blueberry in two and place one half in the middle of the kiwi fruit.
3. With red writing icing, make vein lines round the outside of the kiwi fruit to the edge of the biscuit.

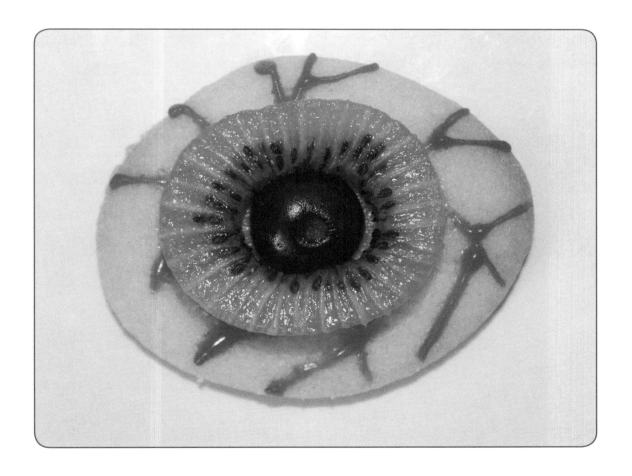

Edible Bible crafts
Festivals

The annunciation

The story

The angel Gabriel went to see Mary, who lived in Nazareth in Galilee. Mary was not much more than a girl but she was engaged to be married to Joseph, the local carpenter.

'Mary,' said Gabriel. 'God is with you!'

Mary was afraid. She didn't know what to think.

'There is no need to be afraid!' said Gabriel. 'You will bear a son and give him the name Jesus. He will be known as God's son and will be a king who will reign for ever!'

'But I am not yet married,' said Mary. 'How can I have a baby?'

'The Holy Spirit will make this happen, for God is able to do anything. Another woman in your family, Elizabeth, is now six months' pregnant. Everyone said that she couldn't have children, but with God, nothing is impossible.'

'I will do anything God wants me to,' said Mary. 'I am ready to serve him in this way.'

Then Gabriel left Mary.

BIBLE REFERENCE: LUKE 1:26–38

> Mary said to the angel, 'How can this be, since I am a virgin?' The angel said to her, 'The Holy Spirit will come upon you, and the power of the Most High will overshadow you; therefore the child to be born will be holy; he will be called Son of God.' (vv. 34–35)

Reflection

The promise of God about the person of Jesus came long before Jesus was actually born. It was a promise that was full of joy and hope, that sang of a deliverer who would rescue the orphan and the widow, lift up the downtrodden and reverse the fortunes of the children of Israel.

All of this hope, this joy, this promise, rested upon the shoulders of a young woman, hardly more than a girl, who was betrothed to a lowly carpenter in an unimportant town in Israel.

This ordinary woman was visited by an angel. What a terrifying thing to happen! Mary's initial reaction was of fear—and once she had conquered her initial fear enough to listen, it must have become even greater, not less at all! She was going to be responsible for the birth of the promised Messiah, the saviour of all her people. But the angel persisted, saying that the power of God would overshadow her and that she should call the child Jesus.

Mary had her life turned upside down by an angel, and her response was to say, 'OK, God, you can be in charge of whatever happens to me.' Everything that was going to happen to her, she accepted, both the good and the bad. There were enormous difficulties: single pregnant women did not have an easy time of it in those days. Her fiancé was deeply troubled by the situation and did not know what to do. Indeed, it took another angel to make him see the right path.

Despite all the difficulties, though, incredible joy came. Throughout the struggles in the years ahead, and even during the final days of Jesus' life on earth, Mary continued to accept God's will for her life and the blessing of joy and peace that came with that acceptance. As we remember the story of Mary's encounter with the angel, let us too commit ourselves to accepting God's will for our lives, whatever that may bring, and pray for the peace that will surely accompany such acceptance.

Reproduced with permission from *Edible Bible Crafts* by Sally Welch, published by Barnabas for Children 2014. www.barnabasinchurches.org.uk

Savoury recipe: Gabriel

Ingredients (per angel)

- One rice cake
- One slice of ham
- Spaghetti cheese
- Scraps of yellow pepper, carrot and black olive

Equipment

- Knife for cutting
- Round cookie cutter

Preparation

None.

Crafting

1. Cut a circle from the ham to make the angel's face.
2. Arrange some spaghetti cheese as hair.
3. Give your angel eyes and a mouth from the olive and carrot or red pepper scraps. If you like, you can cut a halo from the yellow pepper.

Sweet recipe: Gabriel

Note: This is quite a difficult craft and may be too challenging for very young children.

Ingredients (per angel)

- One ice cream cone
- White chocolate or yellow chocolate 'melts'
- White or pink fondant icing
- Edible paper
- Sprinkles and chocolate stars to decorate
- White or yellow writing icing

Equipment

- Scissors

Preparation

If you have time, you can cut the end of the cone off at the point where it starts to widen out. This is not vital but gives a neater angel 'body'.

Melt the chocolate and dip the angel body in until it is completely covered. Leave to dry.

Crafting

1. With the fondant icing, make a round head and push it gently on to the pointed end of the cone.
2. Cover the top of the head with writing icing, then dip it in the sprinkles or other 'angel hair' decoration.
3. Cut a pair of wings from the edible paper and fasten to the angel's back with writing icing.
4. Decorate the angel's gown using writing icing, chocolate stars and sprinkles.

Reproduced with permission from *Edible Bible Crafts* by Sally Welch, published by Barnabas for Children 2014. www.barnabasinchurches.org.uk

Christmas

The story

The months passed quickly and soon the time came for Mary's baby to be born. It looked as though this would not happen in Nazareth, but in Bethlehem.

The Roman emperor, Caesar Augustus, wanted to tax his people. He ordered a census so that everyone had to go to the town of their ancestors to be counted. This meant that Joseph had to take Mary with him to Bethlehem, because he belonged to the family of King David.

Mary and Joseph made their way to the village of Bethlehem in Judea. The roads were full of people travelling, all obeying the commands of their Roman ruler.

Bethlehem was bustling with people. Men, women and children had all come to be registered there. By the time Mary and Joseph arrived, it was already difficult to find somewhere to stay.

Mary felt tired and weary; she was starting to feel the pains that meant her baby would soon be born.

Joseph went from house to house looking for a room because the inn was full. Eventually they found shelter where the animals were stabled.

That night, Mary gave birth to a baby boy, her first-born child. She wrapped him in strips of cloth and made a bed for him in a manger, because there was no room anywhere else.

BIBLE REFERENCE: LUKE 2:1–7

> And she gave birth to her firstborn son and wrapped him in bands of cloth, and laid him in a manger, because there was no place for them in the inn. (v. 7)

Reflection

Throughout the Old Testament, good and evil are in combat with each other. From that first murmur of the serpent in the ears of Adam and Eve, God's wonderful work is under constant threat from the forces of darkness—and it seems as if this will be the case for ever, as the children of Israel fall prey again and again to the temptations of wrongdoing.

God's power will triumph, but not in the way we expect it. Instead of joining in the battle of might, pitting army against army, piling destruction upon chaos, he uses an unexpected strategy, a counter-intuitive strategy that could not be anticipated. A baby is born to an ordinary couple. This child will be the light shining in the darkness of the world. This small creature will put an end to death by his death. He will lead through service and reign in humility. All the assumptions, normalities and brutalities of everyday life are overthrown: might is not right, the battle does not go to the strongest, the first past the post is not the winner. Suddenly the story becomes not one of violence, battle, greed and death, but one of gentleness, humility, peace and great love.

At Christmas, we celebrate the victory of good over evil, the beginning of a new era, a new world, heaven on earth, God's kingdom come. Although the outcome is already decided, individual skirmishes are still being fought, and that's where we come in. Nothing can be as important as the ordinary, the everyday, for that is where life is at its most special. Every action matters: every decision we make for right or wrong, every good word spoken, every helpful deed undertaken, all contribute towards that final glorious victory. It is easy to underestimate the effects of what we do and what we say as we go about our everyday lives. But every little thing counts—every loving word, every prayer—just like the tiny baby, born in a manger, destined to save the world.

Reproduced with permission from *Edible Bible Crafts* by Sally Welch, published by Barnabas for Children 2014. www.barnabasinchurches.org.uk

Savoury recipe: Christmas tree

Ingredients (per tree)

- One slice of bread
- Two sticks of celery
- One slice of processed cheese or one thin slice of cheese
- Tomato or red and yellow pepper (I used Tomberries, but these are quite seasonal, I think)
- Piece of carrot, 5cm long

Equipment

- Knife for cutting
- Very small star cutter

Preparation

You may want to slice the celery for younger children.

Crafting

1. Cut a triangular tree shape from the bread.
2. Cut the celery into thin slices.
3. Cut tiny stars from the cheese, ideally using a star cutter or an icing stamp; it will be tricky freehand.
4. Arrange the celery 'branches' on the bread tree. Decorate the tree with tomato or peppers and cheese stars.
5. Place the carrot at the bottom as a tree stand.

Reproduced with permission from *Edible Bible Crafts* by Sally Welch, published by Barnabas for Children 2014. www.barnabasinchurches.org.uk

Sweet recipe: Jesus

Ingredients (per Jesus)

- One fairy cake
- Chocolate buttercream icing
- White, pink and yellow fondant icing
- A small amount of Shredded Wheat, broken into strands (optional)
- Writing icing or an icing pen

Equipment

- Rolling pin and baking paper
- Large star cutter
- Knife for spreading

Preparation

Younger children may need the yellow fondant icing rolled out and cut into stars for them.

Crafting

1. Spread the chocolate buttercream icing over the top of the fairy cake.
2. Roll out the yellow fondant icing and cut out a star.
3. Place the star on top of the fairy cake. Sprinkle the star and the fairy cake with a little shredded wheat 'straw' (if using).
4. Using the white fondant icing, make a swaddled baby shape. Give the baby a pink head. You can give him features using writing icing or an icing pen.
5. Place the baby gently on the star.

Epiphany

The story

Wise men living in the east had been studying the night skies when Jesus was born. They saw a strange new star and wondered what it could mean.

They set out on a journey, following the star, because they thought it heralded the birth of a new king, and they wanted to worship him.

When they reached Jerusalem, they stopped at King Herod's palace.

'Where is the child born to be king of the Jewish people?' they asked. 'We have come to pay our respects, to welcome and worship him.'

Herod was disturbed by their arrival. What king could there be apart from him? Quickly, Herod consulted the chief priests and teachers of the law. They told him what they knew from the ancient prophecies: the king would be born in Bethlehem.

Herod then talked to his eastern visitors and tried to find out exactly when they had first seen the star. This way he could know how old the baby might be. Then he sent them to Bethlehem.

'If you find the king,' he said craftily, 'let me know. I would like to be able to worship him as well.'

The wise men continued their journey until they reached Bethlehem where the star seemed to stop over a house. They went inside, and found Mary with her young child.

The wise men knew they had found the right place, and worshipped Jesus, the new king. Then they gave him the gifts they had brought—gold, frankincense and myrrh.

They stopped for the night before beginning their return journey, but they did not go back the way they had come. In the night they had dreamed that it was not safe to return to King Herod.

BIBLE REFERENCE: MATTHEW 2:1–12

On entering the house, they saw the child with Mary his mother; and they knelt down and paid him homage. Then, opening their treasure-chests, they offered him gifts of gold, frankincense, and myrrh. And having been warned in a dream not to return to Herod, they left for their own country by another road. (vv. 11–12)

Reflection

One Christmas, a member of our congregation was given not one but three pairs of socks—one silly pair from his sister, one pair of walking socks from his girlfriend and a plain black pair for work from his grandmother. These socks reflected different aspects of his character—the joker, the keen rambler, and the man who had to earn a living. They tell us a story about this man, about who he is, what he does and what he likes. In a similar way, the gifts brought by the magi for Jesus tell us about his character, and we can learn from them.

First was gold, which was a valuable substance even in biblical times. Jesus was born of the royal house of David: he could trace his ancestry back to one of the great Jewish kings. Gold reminds us of his kingship in heaven, despite his humble beginnings on earth. It reminds us that he is the Son of God, with everlasting power, and that he himself chose to limit that power and come and live on earth out of love for us.

Frankincense and myrrh are both resins—dried tree sap—that come from trees of the genus Boswellia (frankincense) and Commiphora (myrhh), which are common to Somalia. The sap is gathered by cutting the tree's bark, causing the sap to ooze out of the cut, which is then allowed to dry on the tree until hard. Worth their weight in gold in ancient times, gifts of frankincense and myrrh were fit for the 'newborn king'. Frankincense had been used for thousands of years before Christ's birth in religious ceremonies to help prayer and meditation. It was given to Jesus as a sign that his birth had not just local or even earthly significance. Like the star that heralded his birth, frankincense reminds us that Jesus' birth was of cosmic significance.

Myrrh injects a spirit of gloom into the festive proceedings, because of its traditional use in anointing and embalming bodies. It reminds us of the inevitability of Jesus' death. However, it also brings the Easter story into the Christmas story, because it reminds us that when the women went to the tomb to anoint Jesus' body, it was not there: Jesus had risen from the dead. By his action we were all released from death.

Just as our friend's pairs of socks highlighted the things his family loved and wanted to affirm about him, so the gifts of the kings stand as reminders to us. They remind us that, despite Jesus' lowly beginnings, he was of royal descent, that his birth has significance not just for us but for the whole universe, and that because of his death we need not fear death.

Savoury recipe: The star

Ingredients (per sky)

- One rice cake
- One slice of processed cheese or one thin slice of cheese
- Marmite

Equipment

- Knife for spreading
- Small star cutters in different sizes

Preparation

None

Crafting

1. Spread Marmite over the rice cake.
2. Using the star cutters, cut out stars from the cheese and place them on the rice cake.

Sweet recipe: The wise men

Note: This is quite a difficult craft and may prove challenging for very young children.

Ingredients (per wise man)

- Pink and yellow fondant icing
- Black writing icing
- Edible paper
- One doughnut ball or cake pop
- One digestive biscuit
- Three American hard gum sweets (these definitely work the best)
- Icing sugar

Equipment

- Rolling pin and baking paper
- Circular cookie cutter
- Knife for cutting

Preparation

1. Place three American hard gums a small distance apart from each other on a piece of baking paper and microwave on medium for 20 seconds at a time until they can be rolled out with a rolling pin. Roll out the sweets using another piece of baking paper on top, until they are big enough for a circle to be cut out of them.
2. Cut out a circle using the cutter. Store separately, after dusting with icing sugar to prevent sticking.

Crafting

1. Stick the doughnut ball or cake pop on to the digestive biscuit using writing icing.
2. Carefully shape the circular hard gum 'gown' over the doughnut ball or cake pop.
3. Make a head from the pink fondant icing and stick it to the gown with writing icing. You can give the wise man features if you like. Make a crown from the yellow fondant icing and place on the head.

Reproduced with permission from *Edible Bible Crafts* by Sally Welch, published by Barnabas for Children 2014. www.barnabasinchurches.org.uk

Ash Wednesday and Lent

The story

After his baptism, Jesus was led by God's Spirit into the desert. He went without food for forty days and at the end of this time Jesus was weak and very hungry.

God's enemy, the devil, tried to test Jesus.

'You need food,' he said. 'If you are God's Son, you can make this stone turn into bread.'

'Life is more than just food,' replied Jesus, quoting God's law.

Then the devil led Jesus to a very high place and showed him all the kingdoms of the world.

'Look at all this!' whispered the devil. 'I will give it to you, if you bow down and worship me.'

'God has said that we must worship him alone,' replied Jesus.

Then the devil took Jesus to Jerusalem. They stood on the highest part of the temple.

'God has promised to send his angels to protect you,' continued the devil. 'Throw yourself off the temple so we can see his power!'

'God's law says that we must not put him to the test,' Jesus replied.

The devil had tried to tempt Jesus to break God's laws and do something wrong, but Jesus would not give in. The devil left and Jesus was alone.

BIBLE REFERENCE: MATTHEW 4:1–11

> Then Jesus was led up by the Spirit into the wilderness to be tempted by the devil. He fasted for forty days and forty nights, and afterwards he was famished. (vv. 1–2)

Reflection

Ash Wednesday and Lent, a period of penitence and fasting, can be difficult to explain to children. But the journey we make through Lent each year gives us an opportunity to examine our motives and priorities in our lives, not just in small matters such as giving up chocolate or alcohol but in the way we order our existence. It is easy to fail: we promise God that we will pray more often, and then we find ourselves so busy that we end up praying less than we have before. We promise God that we will not be so impatient with the annoying people in our lives, and we find ourselves being more impatient than ever. We are tempted; we give in, and we are ashamed. But that is not the end of the story.

Each of us is called to be obedient, to exercise our faith and trust in God's wisdom. It is not a sin to be tempted: indeed, often it is part of God's plan for us. Nor is it a sign that we are lost when we succumb to temptation: Lenten penance may be more effective if we fail in our resolutions than if we succeed, for its purpose is to bring home to us our need for salvation.

What God wants from us is not that we be perfect but that we strive to be that way—we give it our best shot and keep on trying. So this Lent, let us try once more to conform our lives to the life of Christ, and, when we fail (because we will), let us not give up but have faith and grow strong.

Reproduced with permission from *Edible Bible Crafts* by Sally Welch, published by Barnabas for Children 2014. www.barnabasinchurches.org.uk

Savoury recipe: A praying monk

Note: Pretzels are often eaten on Ash Wednesday, as the folds of the pastry look like arms in prayer.

Ingredients (per monk)

- One tortilla
- One slice of brown bread
- One piece of ham
- One black olive
- One pretzel
- Spaghetti cheese (optional)

Equipment

- Knife for cutting
- Small and medium round cutters

Preparation

None.

Crafting

1. Cut a small and a medium circle from the brown bread. Place them on the tortilla to form the monk's head and body.
2. Cut a circle of ham for the monk's face, and give him eyes and a mouth with pieces of olive. If you like, you can make a belt with the spaghetti cheese.
3. Place the 'praying arms' pretzel on the monk's body.

Reproduced with permission from *Edible Bible Crafts* by Sally Welch, published by Barnabas for Children 2014. www.barnabasinchurches.org.uk

Sweet recipe: Ash Wednesday biscuit

Ingredients (per biscuit)

- Two digestive biscuits
- Buttercream icing
- One Oreo cookie

Equipment

- Rolling pin
- Knife for spreading

Preparation

None. (The care needed to make the cross should make this a quiet craft, suitable for Ash Wednesday.)

Crafting

1. Spread buttercream icing over one of the digestive biscuits.
2. Crush the other digestive biscuit with a rolling pin to make fine crumbs. Carefully scatter the biscuit crumbs on to the icing.
3. Crush the Oreo cookie to make fine crumbs. A pinch at a time, carefully sprinkle the Oreo crumbs on to the biscuit to form a cross shape. This echoes the crosses that some people make on their foreheads using the ash from the previous year's palm crosses.

Mothering Sunday

The story

John, one of Jesus' disciples, was standing near the foot of the cross. A group of women, including Jesus' own mother, was also there.

'Dear woman,' Jesus said to Mary, 'treat this man as your son. John,' he then said to his friend, 'treat this woman as if she were your mother.'

BIBLE REFERENCE: JOHN 19:25–27

Meanwhile, standing near the cross of Jesus were his mother, and his mother's sister, Mary the wife of Clopas, and Mary Magdalene. When Jesus saw his mother and the disciple whom he loved standing beside her, he said to his mother, 'Woman, here is your son.' Then he said to the disciple, 'Here is your mother.' And from that hour the disciple took her into his own home.

Reflection

From the beginning of Christianity in England, it was believed that the 'mother church' was the spiritual power that gave life and protected people from harm. It began to be the custom for people to bring gifts to the church and to decorate it with flowers and jewels. By the Middle Ages, the fourth Sunday in Lent was established as a special day to honour the mother church. As a day of celebration, it also provided a day off from the Lenten tradition of fasting and penance.

During the 1600s, this celebration was gradually broadened to include real mothers, and so earned the name Mothering Sunday. Mothering Sunday became an especially compassionate holiday for many English people. Most of the ordinary people of England were employed as servants of wealthy landowners, either as labourers on the land or as servants in the large estate houses. They were therefore forced to live away from their homes, often in the homes of their employers. On this fourth Sunday in Lent, Mothering Sunday, they were allowed to return to the place of their birth and visit their families for a day. Often they took small gifts or a 'mothering cake' also known as simnel cake.

The earliest simnel cakes were like biscuits in their size, texture and thinness, but today the simnel cake is more likely to be a rich fruit cake covered with a thick layer of almond paste or icing. The cake may be topped with eleven marzipan balls, representing Jesus' disciples, excluding Judas.

Earlier traditions saw the cake being eaten on this day, but it soon became customary to keep the cake until Easter Sunday. Keeping the cake stored for the weeks leading up to Easter was seen to be a test of a young girl's culinary skills: she was considered to be a good cook if the cake retained its taste and moistness on Easter Sunday.

There are lots of different ways to celebrate mothers, but fundamentally they are all saying the same thing: 'I love you and value you. Thank you for sharing your life with me.' It is true that occasions such as Mother's Day are greatly commercialised but they do provide an opportunity that we might otherwise miss for telling our mothers that we love them. Let us remember to say this in as many ways as we can, reflecting the love of the one who first loved us.

Reproduced with permission from *Edible Bible Crafts* by Sally Welch, published by Barnabas for Children 2014. www.barnabasinchurches.org.uk

Savoury recipe: A flower

Ingredients (per flower)

- One rice cake
- Cucumber or carrot
- Red or green or yellow pepper

Equipment

- Knife for slicing

Preparation

Small children may need the cucumber or carrot sliced for them.

Crafting

1. Slice the cucumber as thinly as you can, then cut the slices in half.
2. Arrange the half slices on the rice cake in a spiral to look like flower petals.
3. Make a centre out of a slice of carrot. Alternatively, use carrot slices as petals and make a centre from pepper.

Sweet recipe: A flower

Ingredients (per flower)

- One fairy cake
- Buttercream icing
- Mini marshmallows
- Sugar crystals or other decoration

Equipment

- Scissors
- Knife for spreading

Preparation

Younger children may need help to cut the marshmallows. This cannot be done too far in advance or the marshmallows will get sticky.

Crafting

1. Spread the buttercream icing over the top of the fairy cake.
2. With the scissors, cut the mini marshmallows in half diagonally.
3. Dip the cut surface of each half in sugar crystals. Arrange the half marshmallows on the fairy cake as petals.

Easter

The story

After the Sabbath, at dawn on the first day of the week, Mary Magdalene and the other Mary went to look at the tomb.

There was a violent earthquake, for an angel of the Lord came down from heaven and, going to the tomb, rolled back the stone and sat on it. His appearance was like lightning, and his clothes were white as snow. The guards were so afraid of him that they shook and became like dead men.

The angel said to the women, 'Do not be afraid, for I know that you are looking for Jesus, who was crucified. He is not here; he has risen, just as he said. Come and see the place where he lay. Then go quickly and tell his disciples: "He has risen from the dead and is going ahead of you into Galilee. There you will see him." Now I have told you.'

So the women hurried away from the tomb, afraid yet filled with joy, and ran to tell his disciples. Suddenly Jesus met them. 'Greetings,' he said. They came to him, clasped his feet and worshipped him. Then Jesus said to them, 'Do not be afraid. Go and tell my brothers to go to Galilee; there they will see me.'

BIBLE REFERENCE: MATTHEW 28:1–10 (NIV)

> The angel said to the women, 'Do not be afraid; for I know that you are looking for Jesus, who was crucified. He is not here; he has risen, just as he said. Come and see the place where he lay.' (vv. 5–6)

Reflection

My son was not very well when he was born. The doctors had spotted a defect during an ultrasound scan and that set off a whole battery of tests, some very painful. Finally we came to get the results of the test for the most serious condition he might have. We sat in the consultant's room and he looked at the tests and said, 'Well, Mr and Mrs Welch, this one's all clear.'

'All clear'—two words that put an end to worrying, fear, hours spent waiting in hospitals or looking up into the dark in the middle of the night. 'All clear.'

There are other phrases, both good and bad, that are equally powerful: 'I'm pregnant'; 'I love you'; 'We've lost him'. Entire life stories are built up around these life-changing words.

At Easter we celebrate some of the most important words in the Christian story: 'He is not here, for he has been raised.' Just like the other words, they change lives. Almost as soon as they have been spoken, they start their transforming work.

The first to be changed were the women, who had arrived at the tomb at dawn. Perhaps this was the earliest time they were allowed out of their homes after the sabbath, or it could be that if they were up and about at dawn, there was less chance that they would be discovered, for they were frightened women. They had come to bury the person who had seemed to offer them a new life, a new way of living—someone who gave them love, healing and an insight into the ways of God. But they did not believe enough, they did not trust in his words, and so they had come, full of mourning and grief, to bury him.

They were met by an angel sitting among the bandages in which Jesus had been wrapped, who shared with them the words that would help them to begin new lives, full of joy, with a future totally different from the one they had expected. Thanks to these words, we can look, with those two women and with countless others, to a new life, full of assurance and joy.

Savoury recipe: A chick

Ingredients (per chick)

- One tortilla
- One slice of bread
- One slice of processed cheese
- One black olive
- A piece of carrot
- Some lettuce

Equipment

- Large and small oval cookie cutters (or round plastic cutters squashed into an oval shape)
- Knife for cutting

Preparation

Young children may need help with the chick's beak and eyes.

Crafting

1. Cut an oval from the cheese slice, using the large cutter, and place it on the tortilla.
2. Cut the same sized oval from the bread slice, then cut the oval in half horizontally. Cut the straight edge to form zigzags, as if it is a broken egg shell.
3. Cut a smaller oval from the cheese slice, using the other cutter. Cut this oval in half diagonally to form wings.
4. Place the cheese wings on the chick, then put the bread eggshell on top.
5. Cut a beak from the carrot slice. Cut two eyes from the olive. Place them on the chick's face and surround the chick with shredded lettuce 'straw'.

Reproduced with permission from *Edible Bible Crafts* by Sally Welch, published by Barnabas for Children 2014. www.barnabasinchurches.org.uk

Sweet recipe: Easter biscuits

Ingredients (per biscuit)

- One egg-shaped biscuit (see recipe on page 16)
- Chocolate
- Writing icing

Equipment

- None

Preparation

Heat the chocolate in the microwave on medium heat, in 20-second bursts, until melted. Do not overheat or the chocolate will become gritty and difficult to use.

Note: If it is difficult to use melted chocolate in your craft area, bring the biscuits ready coated with chocolate, then decorate with writing icing.

Crafting

1. Dip the bottom half of the biscuit in melted chocolate.
2. While the chocolate is setting, decorate the rest of the biscuit with writing icing.

Pentecost

The story

Jerusalem was full of visitors from all over the world. They had come for the festival of Pentecost.

The believers were together in one room when, suddenly, a sound like a strong wind blew through the house, filling it with noise. Something like flames seemed to burn in the air and touch each person there. As the Holy Spirit touched them, they all began to speak in other languages.

The noise from the house attracted a crowd. 'What's happening?' some of them said. 'I can understand what these men are saying. They are speaking in my language, talking about God. How is this possible?'

'They're drunk!' laughed others.

'No, we're not!' said Peter, coming out to speak to the crowd. 'It's only nine o'clock in the morning.' Then Peter stood up to teach all those who would listen.

First, Peter reminded them of what the prophets had told them would happen. Then he told them about Jesus, God's chosen one, the Messiah. When Peter described how Jesus had been arrested and beaten and then put to death, the people were horrified.

'What shall we do?' they asked.

'You must turn away from your sins and be baptised,' Peter told them. 'Then you can be forgiven, and you will receive the Holy Spirit as we have.'

That day 3000 people became followers of Jesus. The apostles performed many miracles in the name of Jesus, and they met together with the other believers to worship God, to pray and to share what they had with each other.

BIBLE REFERENCE: ACTS 2:1–41

> Divided tongues, as of fire, appeared among them, and a tongue rested on each of them. All of them were filled with the Holy Spirit and began to speak in other languages, as the Spirit gave them ability. (vv. 3–4)

Reflection

Pentecost celebrates the birthday of the church, the way it all started with the experience of the disciples of Jesus 50 days after his departure. These frightened people, gathered together in one room for fear of persecution, were touched by fire and wind—the Holy Spirit—and began to do things that they had never done before. They were made new, created again in the Spirit of God.

This small group left their safety and shelter and moved out among the people, to share the good news of God's love with them. They reached out in love to all they met, filled with the power of the Spirit.

The Holy Spirit is still here, still working. Sometimes we forget that, as we are so preoccupied with our own struggles. In England, about one person in every twelve goes to church at least once a month. One person in twelve, spread throughout the population, is trying to live a gospel life, sharing gospel values. We can do a lot in our communities, because there *are* enough of us. All we need to do is let the Spirit work in us and through us, releasing the power of Christ into the world.

At a confirmation service I attended, the bishop talked about the reactions of people when they look in a pram at a baby: they comment on how beautiful the baby is or how lovely. He said that this is what God does when he sees us: he sees how wonderful we are. The bishop went on to ask everyone in the congregation to look at each other in that light, to see the beauty inside that God sees, acknowledging and forgiving the faults and appreciating the best bits. That is what we need to do in our church

Reproduced with permission from *Edible Bible Crafts* by Sally Welch, published by Barnabas for Children 2014. www.barnabasinchurches.org.uk

community. We need to look at it realistically, acknowledging its faults and weaknesses, but still gazing on it with love and adoration. It is a beautiful church. We are beautiful people.

Savoury recipe: Pentecost candle

Ingredients (per candle)

- One bread roll
- One carrot
- Some red pepper

Equipment

- Round cookie cutter
- Knife for cutting

Preparation

None.

Crafting

1. Cut the top off the bread roll. Using the cutter, cut a circle out from the bottom half.
2. Cut a smaller circle from the centre of the roll, the same size as the end of the carrot.
3. Shape the carrot so that it can stand in the bread circle 'candlestick'.
4. Cut a flame shape from the red pepper.
5. Cut a small notch in the top of the candle and insert the red pepper flame.

Sweet recipe: Dove

Ingredients (per dove)

- One fairy cake
- Red fondant icing
- White fondant icing
- Yellow fondant icing or a jelly diamond

Equipment

- Circular cookie cutters

Preparation

It is probably best to cut out all the circles beforehand unless the children are old enough to roll out quite a lot of fondant icing.

Note: It is important to have a ready-made example for this craft or it could get confusing.

Crafting

1. From the red icing, cut a circle the same circumference as the top of the fairy cake.
2. From the white icing, cut two smaller circles of different sizes for the head and body of the dove. If you wish, you can cut out a small piece from the larger circle so that the head fits neatly on to the body, but it is fine if one simply rests on the other.
3. Cut an oval shape from the white icing for the wing.
4. Either cut a small triangular beak from the yellow icing or cut the jelly diamond in half as a beak.
5. Assemble the shapes on top of the fairy cake to look like a dove.

Reproduced with permission from *Edible Bible Crafts* by Sally Welch, published by Barnabas for Children 2014. www.barnabasinchurches.

Harvest

The story

God looked at everything that he had made and saw that it was good.

Then God made man and woman. He put them in charge of his creation, to care for it and cultivate it for food. God loved the people he had made and he saw that everything he had made was very good. Then God rested.

God gave Adam and Eve a beautiful garden to live in. It was full of plants and trees with fruit they could eat. The garden was watered by a river that ran through it and Adam and Eve tended the garden and worked in it.

Adam and Eve were good company for each other. They shared the work and they lived happily together.

BIBLE REFERENCE: GENESIS 1:26–31

> God said, 'See, I have given you every plant yielding seed that is upon the face of all the earth, and every tree with seed in its fruit; you shall have them for food.' (v. 29)

Reflection

There is an old fable told about a far-off land that was ruled by a tyrant. The tyrant had an iron grip over all parts of his kingdom, except for one frustrating area where he was unable to destroy the people's belief in God.

He summoned his counsellors and put the question to them, 'Where can I hide God so that the people will end up forgetting him?' One counsellor suggested that God be hidden on the dark side of the moon. This proposal was debated for some time, but was voted down because it was believed that one day scientists would discover a means of space travel and God would end up being found again.

Another adviser to the tyrant came up with the idea of burying God beneath the depths of the ocean floor. This was voted down for the same reason: it was felt that scientific advancement would lead to the discovery of God even beneath the depths of the ocean floor.

Finally the oldest and wisest of the counsellors had a flash of insight. 'I know,' he said, 'why don't we hide God where no one will ever think of finding him?' He explained, 'If we hide God in the ordinary events of people's everyday lives, they'll never find him.' And so it was done—and they say that the people are still looking for God, even today.

At harvest time, we see God and what he does in the normal and routine parts of our lives a little more clearly than we normally do. After all, what could be more routine than food, its purchase, preparation and consumption?

So that is why we have harvest festivals—to give us a short space in our lives just to sit back and be thankful. The Bible readings focus on what God has done, and the decorations in the church echo the beauty of the countryside and help us towards an appreciation of God's creation and all that we have to be thankful for.

...ission from *Edible Bible Crafts* by Sally Welch,
...ldren 2014. www.barnabasinchurches.org.uk

Savoury recipe: Basket

Ingredients (per basket)

- One crusty or other bread roll
- One carrot
- One cherry tomato
- Some cauliflower
- Other miniature vegetables

Equipment

- Knife for cutting

Preparation

None.

Crafting

1. Cut the top off the roll. Remove the inside from the remainder of the roll. This will be your harvest basket.
2. Arrange miniature vegetables in the basket. You can cut the carrot into smaller shapes. It is a good idea if you have several to choose from, to introduce the idea of selecting the best as a gift for God.

119

Sweet recipe: Vegetable patch

Ingredients (per patch)

- One fairy cake
- Chocolate buttercream icing
- One Oreo cookie
- Coloured fondant icing

Equipment

- None

Preparation

Crush the Oreo cookies until they look like soil.

Crafting

1. Spread the the buttercream icing over the fairy cake.
2. Sprinkle the Oreo cookie 'soil' over the icing.
3. Using the coloured fondant icing, mould different vegetables for your garden.

Also from Barnabas for Children

• •

The Barnabas Children's Bible

Rhona Davies

Illustrated by Marcin Piwowarski

This Children's Bible includes stories chosen to cover all the main events, retold with a continuous thread.

There are 365 stories, one for every day of the year, each accompanied by Bible quotations from a real Bible translation, giving readers a taste of the language and style of the original texts.

The stylish illustrations illuminate and inform, while the easily accessible encyclopedia at the end of the book helps to explain the context and background of the stories. All combine to make this a useful and readable Bible for children.

ISBN 978 0 85746 081 3   £12.99

Available from your local Christian bookshop or direct from BRF: visit www.brfonline.org.uk

Also from Barnabas for Children

• •

Encyclopedia of Bible Crafts

187 fun-filled, easy-to-do craft activities for children

Laurie Castañeda

Children love doing craft activities—and children's leaders love crafts that connect children to Bible truths! This bumper collection of creative, fun-filled and easy-to-do Bible crafts is designed to inspire and enthuse leaders and children alike as they explore the Bible together.

Each tried-and-tested craft is designed to fit into any Bible-based children's work programme, whether that's on a Sunday, midweek, or a one-off special event. Every single book of the Bible is covered, with crafts to illustrate many key Bible passages. The crafts are easy to prepare, easy to do and require very little equipment or materials.

Alongside the craft activities you will also find:

- An age guide for each craft
- A Bible reference
- A Bible point
- 'You will need' list
- Handy hints
- Step-by-step instructions
- Teaching point

ISBN 978 0 85746 217 6   £12.99
Available from your local Christian bookshop or direct from BRF: visit www.brfonline.org.uk

Also from Barnabas for Children

• •

Paper Plate Bible Crafts

58 easy-to-do ideas for 5–7s

Anita Reith Stohs

Paper Plate Bible Crafts is a great resource for fun crafts that teach favourite Bible stories in any setting.

Fast, inexpensive and readily available, paper plates easily become masks, mobiles, puppets and plaques. The finished crafts are an ingenious way to reinforce Bible stories and themes.

The book includes 58 tried and tested ideas for 5–7s, each with simple templates and easy-to-follow instructions. Alongside the paper plate, each craft uses basic, everyday materials such as card, felt-tipped pens, scissors and glue and can be completed as suggested or adapted to suit the needs and skills of the children.

Each craft idea includes:

- Key Bible story reference
- Full equipment list
- Easy-to-follow instructions
- Simple discussion starters
- Alternative ideas for making the craft
- Illustration of the finished craft

ISBN 978 0 85746 261 9   £7.99
Available from your local Christian bookshop or direct from BRF: visit www.brfonline.org.uk

Also from Barnabas for Children

• •

Fill the Gap!

120 instant Bible games for Sunday schools and midweek groups

Rebecca Parkinson

Fill the Gap! contains 120 easy-to-play Bible-based games with little or no preparation needed—perfect for picking straight off the shelf. The ideas are designed to help local churches fill up those awkward gaps of time in Sunday schools, midweek clubs, holiday clubs, after-school clubs and children's camps.

The games are divided equally across the Old Testament and the New Testament and offer a fun-filled way to reinforce a teaching point or help children who are unfamiliar with Bible stories. There are two games for each story, one aimed at 4–7s and the other at 7–11s, but many of the games can be modified slightly to make them appropriate for older or younger children to take part.

Most of the games are suitable for both smaller and larger groups of children and many can be easily adapted to fit different Bible stories, allowing favourite games to be used again with a different emphasis.

ISBN 978 0 85746 004 2   £8.99

Available from your local Christian bookshop or direct from BRF: visit www.brfonline.org.uk

From Messy Church

• •

Messy Crafts

A craft-based journal for Messy Church members

Lucy Moore

This book is a craft book with a difference! As well as bulging with craft ideas to inspire your creativity at Messy Church, it is also a journal to scribble in, doodle on and generally make your own.

The intention is that it will become a scrapbook of conversations, messy moments and prayers—a part of everyday life at home where you can sketch in your own ideas, list useful websites, make notes, reflect on spiritual moments, and journal your Messy Church journey.

'What excites me about this publication in particular is the format and layout, the visual prompts and references that act as a catalyst to turbo-charge the possibilities around messy spaces.'
FROM THE FOREWORD BY MARLENE WYLIE

ISBN 978 0 85746 068 4   £6.99
Available from your local Christian bookshop or direct from BRF: visit www.brfonline.org.uk

Enjoyed
this book?

Write a review—we'd love to hear what you think. Email: reviews@brf.org.uk

Keep up to date—receive details of our new books as they happen.
Sign up for email news and select your interest groups at:
www.brfonline.org.uk/findoutmore/

Follow us on Twitter @brfonline

By post—to receive new title information by post (UK only), complete the form below and post to: BRF Mailing Lists, 15 The Chambers, Vineyard, Abingdon, Oxfordshire, OX14 3FE

Your Details

Name _____

Address_____

_____

Town/City _____ Post Code _____

Email _____

Your Interest Groups (*Please tick as appropriate)

- ☐ Advent/Lent
- ☐ Bible Reading & Study
- ☐ Children's Books
- ☐ Discipleship
- ☐ Leadership
- ☐ Messy Church
- ☐ Pastoral
- ☐ Prayer & Spirituality
- ☐ Resources for Children's Church
- ☐ Resources for Schools

Support your local bookshop
Ask about their new title information schemes.